For more copies of this book contact us through our website:
www.lifeapplicationbibleseminar.com

Quantity discounts are available for churches and bible study groups.

Before you start to read this book, acquire a Life Application Bible, they are meant to be used together.

Edited By: Patricia Moffett and Chris Moffett
Cover Design: Chris Moffett
ISBN: 978-0-9842934-1-4

This book is dedicated

To all those who have encouraged us to follow our dream and use the Life Application Bible in the mission field.
We especially want to acknowledge the inspiration we have received from the life of
Dr. Kenneth N. Taylor,
Translator of the Living Bible & founder of Tyndale House Publishers.
Dr. Taylor had a life long passion for God's Word and a vision for the Bible to be accessible to all people in all languages. A pioneer in this area, he worked to provide and distribute Bibles around the world.
Also special thanks to
Mr. Mark Taylor, President of Tyndale House Publishers,
who suggested we write a book on how to use the Life Application Bible based on our experience in the mission field.
The result is this book.

Psalms 16:3 "How excellent are the Lord's faithful people! My greatest pleasure is to be with them

Special thanks to our marvelous comrades:

Dick & Sue Bontke, Anne and Marcus Jones, esq of Sierra Leone; Pastor Ray Hosein, LAB Seminar Caribbean Coordinator; Bonnie Cain, Tyndale House Publishers; Dr. Bruce Barton, Mitzie Barton, Scot Barton, Livingstone Corp; Dale Coad, Director AGWM; Freddy Biesum, Teen Challenge Aruba; Pastor Theo Orman, Aruba; Pastor Tim Concannon, Chaplin Jerome Smith, Pastor Nancy Palmer, Pastor Diana Rehill. Missionaries: Sharon Cattell; Carole Frawley; Terry Weist; Joseph & MaryAnne Schaffner; Barry B. Bramble, Esq; Michael Vassalotti; Domingo Rivera; Lisa & Werner Goerke, Timothy Lunsford, Bobbie Cox, Bob Andrews, Margarita Caban, David & Kathy Clark, Aaron Taylor Clark, MD, Bill & Kristie Hickman, Victoria Hickman, Frank DeBellis, Pat & Denise McCleary, John C. Moyer, Mike Ritter, Pam Tippins, William & Theresa Coaxum, Doug & Debbie Vail.

TABLE OF CONTENTS WITH OVERVIEW

Below is an expanded and in-depth Table of Contents. It has been written at the request of many pastors and church leaders we have had the privilege of serving around the world. They have asked for a simplified and clear list of the important information found in this book. This list is designed to help locate key charts, study guides, stories and other resources at a glance. It is essential that you take time to become familiar with this Table of Contents. Understanding the material, its flow and progression, will help you grasp the information in this book and in the Life Application Bible.

You can earn a diploma. As an individual or part of a study group you can receive a diploma by completing the course in this book with a designated seminar instructor in your area or an internet seminar instructor. You must complete all exercises, write in your reflections and answer all questions found on pages 35; 37; 39; 42-44; 53; 57-58; 63-64; 67-68; 90; 116-117; 124; 137-138.

Note: Words underlined and in italics indicates a story. The story illustrates a key point being made in that section of the book.

The following section, from pages 161 to 168, is a must read section where vital terms, summaries and resources are covered

COMPELLING MOTIVES

SEND ME ONE HUNDRED WISE MEN OF THE CHRISTIAN FAITH

In 1269 Kublai Khan sent a request from Peking to Rome asking for one hundred wise men of the Christian faith. Then he said, "and so I shall be baptized, and when I shall be baptized all my barons and great men shall be baptized, and all their subjects will be baptized, and so there will be more Christians here than there are where you are. That was a time when the Mongols were wavering in the choice of their religion. It might have been, as Kublai Khan predicted, the greatest mass religious movement the world has ever seen. The history of all Asia and possibly the world would have been changed. But what actually happened? Pope Gregory X answered by sending two Dominican friars. They went as far as Armenia; they could endure no longer and returned home.

And so passed one of the greatest missionary opportunities in the history of the world.

Let us never again miss an opportunity, great or small, that can change this world for Christ!

THE GOAL OF THIS BOOK

Ephesians 4:11 He Himself gave some to be apostles, prophets, evangelists, pastors and teachers to equip the saints for the work of ministry that the body of Christ may be built up.

We strongly believe in the power of God's Word to affect and change lives. We acknowledge that the help and guidance of the Holy Spirit as our Teacher is essential.

Our goal in writing this book is

a. to equip you for the work of ministry.
b. to encourage you as church leaders, pastors, teachers and others to study, understand and apply God's Word at a deeper level.
c. to help you effectively understand and use the resources of the Life Application Bible.
d. to prepare you to teach these same principles to others.

Photo by Andrew Moffett

THE TREASURE HUNTER'S GUIDE TO THE LIFE APPLICATION BIBLE

Psalm 119:111 proclaims: Your Words are a treasure. They are truly my heart's delight.
Psalm 119:162 also says: I rejoice in Your Word like one who finds a great treasure.

"Over the past thirteen years we have conducted Life Application Bible Seminars in more than fifteen countries, teaching many how to use this wonderful tool. We have found unbelievable treasure, riches and blessings in the Word of God and the Life Application Bible. Scripture, charts, footnotes, personality profiles and more, insights that have so blessed us and helped us grow spiritually, we felt compelled to share them with others, so that the blessings and treasure would be multiplied. This book is an effort to share these treasures. Enter into it, read, study, takes notes, answer the questions, use it to share with others what you have found. The blessing of God's Word has no end or limit. As you give it away God will multiply it back to you. Good measure, pressed down and overflowing. Have no doubt; God's blessings will be upon you as you take out His Word. Be sure to reflect on and enjoy the many pictures of Christian brothers and sisters who have sought and found the treasure of God's Word in the Life Application Bible and through our seminars."
~Jim Moffett

A BRIEF EXPLANATION OF THE LIFE APPLICATION BIBLE

The treasure we speak of is the Life Application Bible.

a. It is the number one selling study Bible in the world.
b. It is a small Bible library in one book.
c. It has been called a "Teacher's Resource Bible" and a "Bible College in a book".
d. It is the work of more than one hundred Bible scholars.
e. It provides a conservative faith-filled commentary on Scripture with ten thousand footnotes for personal life application, character studies, timelines, maps, charts, diagrams, textual notes and indexes.
f. It has been studied and applied bringing revival to many individuals and churches around the world.
g. It is easy to use when its features are explained and understood. You don't need to know the whole Bible, but you do need to understand how to access and locate the information you seek.

We come to share the Life Application Bible so that you too will be enriched in receiving, just as we are enriched by the privilege of bringing God's Word to you.

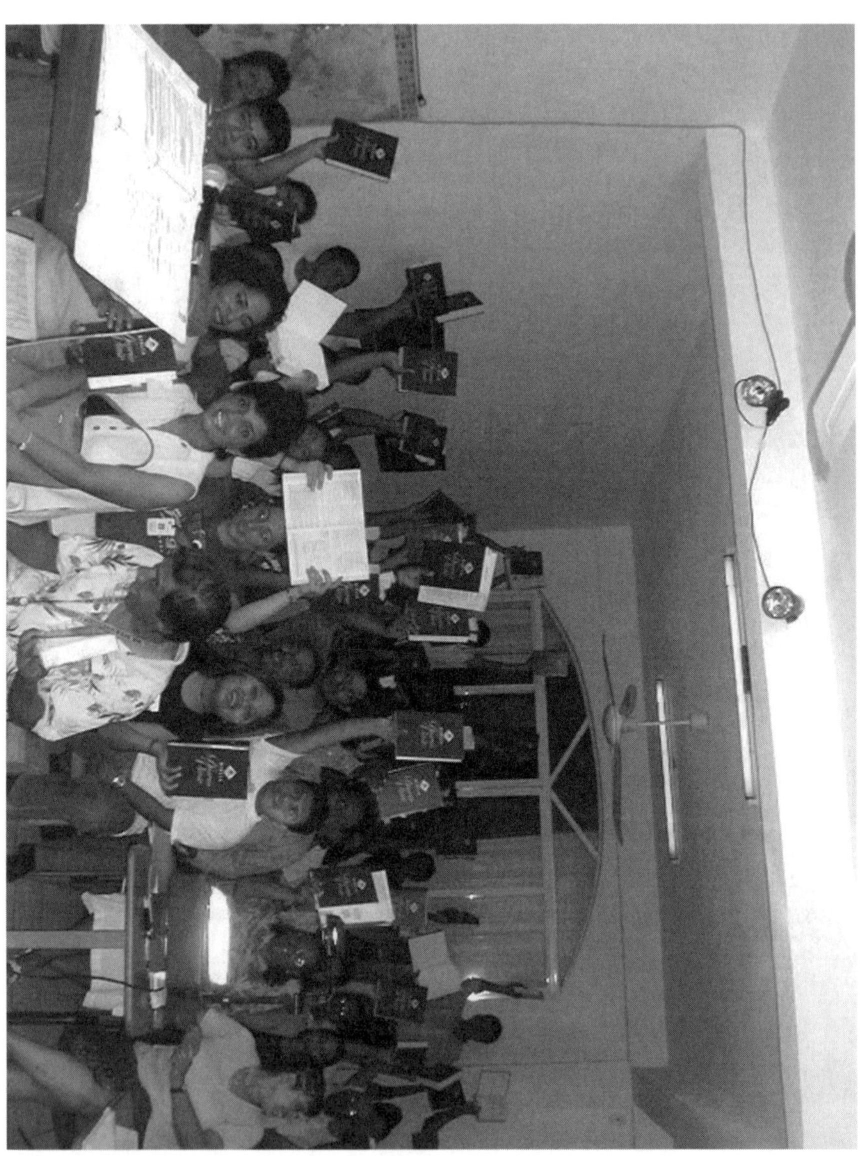

Ministerio
Internacional
Mi Vina

WILL YOU BE PART OF THE LEGACY?

Get in the flow of the Gospel. It is like a mighty river flowing out from Christ and the Cross. Some Christians only stand on the bank and observe as others dive into the flow and take the Gospel to hungry hearts. Those who will take it out experience the power and exhilaration; the life force and satisfaction that were experienced by Jesus and the apostles. They enter a realm of Christianity that is open to all, but only a few experience. They know the life of the soldier on the frontlines with Jesus. It is part of the essence of the Christian life.

You were born for such a time as this. You have the call and the command of the Savior and the same Spirit that filled Him dwells in you. Don't miss it. You have an amazing tool and weapon in the Life Application Bible to evangelize, to disciple and to build the Kingdom.

With this handbook, using the Life Application Bible is made easy and understandable. All the instruction you need is made clear and available. Dive in and you become part of the legacy of the spreading of God's Word to the nations. Your success will be written in heaven where victories for Christ are celebrated eternally.

The Life Application Bible Seminar has been conducted in the following locations:

Aruba (Oranjested)
Cuba (Havana)
Curacao (Willemsted)
Dominican Republic (Azua, La Romano, Santiago,
Santo Domingo)
Ecuador (Cuenca, Quayaquil)
El Salvador (San Salvador)
Fiji (Lombasa, Nandi, Suva)
Ghana (Accra, Kumasi, Tamale)
Grenada (Sauteurs, St. George)
Guyana (Georgetown)
Honduras (LaCeiba, Olanchito, Roatan Island, Tegulcigalpa)
Mexico (Cozumel, Juarez, Valladolid,
Yucatan Peninsula—Xcan)
Nicaragua (Leone, Managua)
Sierra Leone (Bo, Freetown,)
St. Lucia (Castries, Vieux Fort)
Trinidad (Chaguanas, Port of Spain, San Fernando, 5 Prisons)
Uganda
Venezuela (Barquisemeto, Cabimas, Coro, Punto Fijo)

United States
Palmyra, NJ (Leadership Training Seminars)
Recovery Houses NJ, PA, DE & NY
(Teen Challenge Philadelphia, PA; Brooklyn, NY; Long Island, NY; House of Adonai, Philadelphia, PA; City Team Ministries, Chester, PA; Victory Outreach; My Brother's Keeper)
Montana State and Federal Prisons
Blackfeet Indian Nation, Montana
Philadelphia, PA Prison System

HOW TO GET THE MOST OUT OF THIS BOOK

- Read the Glossary in the back of the book and become familiar with the terms and definitions
- Circle, underline, use Post-it-Notes to mark key places as you read
- Complete all exercises and home study challenges
- Write down your thoughts and reflections in the spaces provided. Your reflections and discoveries are the easiest to share with others
- Plan to share with at least one other person the riches of God's Word you discover

There is a Kenyan proverb that says, **"It is a crime in the desert if you know where the oasis is and do not tell others."** We have found in the Life Application Bible an oasis that everyone can drink from. We are compelled to tell others.

CHAPTER 1

WINNING THE BATTLE OF THE MIND
(Change your thinking)
HOW DO YOU SEE YOURSELF?

THE IQ SCORES

In the 1960's a teacher was given a list showing the actual IQ test scores of the students of one class, and for another class a list in which the IQ column had been mistakenly filled in with the student's locker numbers. When the lists were posted at the beginning of the semester the teacher assumed that the locker numbers were the actual IQ's of the students. After a year it was discovered that in the first class the students with high actual IQ scores had performed better than those with low ones but in the second class the students with higher locker numbers scored significantly higher than those with lower locker numbers.

The teacher saw the students differently and presumed they had high IQ's. The students saw themselves differently, encouraged by the teacher.

Proverbs 23:7 As a man thinketh in his heart, so he is.
The Great Teacher, Jesus, sees you differently (to Him you all have high spiritual IQ's). Will you finally start to see yourself as the Teacher sees you and start performing your work for Him at that new level of excellence?

Add your reflections here:

____

____

____

____

____

Many times before we begin a Life Application Bible Course we must bring down some of the walls of wrong thinking built up over the years. Often people have feelings of inadequacy, inability and unbelief that God can use them to teach, share and minister with the Life Application Bible.

- I don't have enough education (neither did the apostles)
- You don't understand, I can't speak well in public (God provided an Aaron for Moses, until Moses learned to do well on his own)
- But I'm fearful (so was Gideon until he heard God call him a mighty warrior)
- I'm only a woman (look what God accomplished through Queen Esther)

When all is said and done…it's not by might and not by power but by the Spirit of the Lord that great things are accomplished. God will make up for whatever you lack in ability. All He asks for is your availability.

It's important to believe that God uses ordinary people like you and I.

When you feel God can't use you, it's helpful to remember… Noah was a drunk; Abraham was too old; Isaac was a daydreamer; Jacob was a liar; Leah was ugly; Joseph was abused; Moses had a stuttering problem; Gideon was afraid; Samson had long hair and was a womanizer; Rahab was a prostitute; Jeremiah and Timothy were too young; David had an affair and was a murderer; Elijah was suicidal; Isaiah preached naked; Jonah ran from God; Naomi was a widow; Job went bankrupt; Peter denied Christ; the Disciples fell asleep while praying; Martha worried about everything; the Samaritan woman was divorced, more than once; Zaccheus was too small; Paul was too religious; Timothy had an stomach problem AND Lazarus was dead!

1 Corinthians 1:27-29 God chose the weak and the foolish of this world to shame the wise and the strong…..so that mankind can do no boasting before God.

If you still think you're not qualified **ask yourself these questions…**

Are you married? Do you have children? Do you have neighbors? Do you shop for groceries? Do you have co-workers? Then **you are somebody's primary teacher**. Some time, somewhere God will use you to share His Word with someone. The more you study the Life Application Bible, the more prepared you will be.

Consider the following list that we call **The Power of One**. It contains wonderful testimonies about how God can use ordinary people like you and I to accomplish great things. Be encouraged as you read it. God is no respecter of persons. He can and will use you to do a mighty work.

THE POWER OF ONE LIFE APPLICATION BIBLE

Many times we are tempted to look at the many Life Application Bibles going forth to the nations and overlook the power of just one. God's Word tells us

- Zechariah 4:10 Do not despise the day of small beginnings.
  Each Life Application Bible in the hands of a believer is another small beginning.

- Isaiah 55:10-11 My Word shall not return to Me void, says the Lord, but shall go forth and fulfill the purpose for which I have sent it.
  Let us not forget that each Life Application Bible because it is God's Word, has God's victory power built into it to accomplish His purpose.

We have received the following testimonies about the power of just one Life Application Bible in the hands of God's people.

- **A pastor in the Fiji Islands**: I have a church of over 2000 people. I have never had such a tool as this to teach them. This Bible will feed us and nurture our people for years to come.
- **A director of a drug and alcohol recovery house**: This Bible you gave me is fantastic. Knowing God's Word explained in footnotes, charts and study materials in this Bible will be a key to maintaining sobriety for our people.
- **Two pastors in a communist country** with only one Life Application Bible between them take turns using it to prepare sermons and Bible studies. One Bible is feeding two congregations.
- **A student** who completed a Life Application Bible Seminar and received his own Bible went back to his home, the Island of Aruba, and spiritually set a fire in the hearts of many. As a result, we were asked to do two

seminars on that island, as well as visit neighboring islands and take the Life Application Bible and Seminar to Venezuela.

- **Mary, a secretary on an island in the South Pacific**, received a Life Application Bible and completed Seminar. Although she had no formal training, she was able to start a Bible study in her home village and lead many to Christ.
- **A Bible College in Africa** received one Life Application Bible for their library. Daily the students took their turn studying it and preparing lessons for their classes.
- **A pastor in South Africa** used his Life Application Bible daily. Tragically his life was ended by a shot fired in a riot. His bible was handed on to another pastor who carried on the work.

As a single Life Application Bible goes out into the hands of believers, we must remember

- God is moving behind the scenes preparing the way for His Word to go forth and be received in the hearts of others.
- God will make possible divine appointments and Holy Spirit encounters to further the ministry of His Word.
- His Word will cause chain reactions and ripple effects touching thousands of people and impacting nations.

DILIGENT STUDY (Study to show yourself approved unto God… 2 Timothy 2:15)
Diligently studying and knowing the Life Application Bible is a most important preparation. Knowing this bible can help you deal with the problems, trials and challenges of life. It can also prepare you to help others with wisdom from God's Word.
We ask all who want to be successful in using the Life Application Bible to **here and now make a firm commitment** to faithfully study and apply yourself to learning all the insights this book has to offer. Take notes and write down your reflections as you read.

A story comes to mind on the need for preparation.

- ***The Girl on the Bridge***

  A young man was on his way home from work in a mid-western city. While he was crossing a bridge he noticed a car coming in the other direction. The car abruptly stopped and a young lady got out. She went to the edge of the bridge and started to climb over the rail. He jumped out of his car and ran towards her, pleading with her not to take her life. When he got near to her she leaped over the side and into the water. He was moved with compassion. Without giving it a thought, he jumped over the rail to save her. The river was deep and wide. On the way down the young man realized that he could not swim. He hit the water and began to struggle. The girl, already in the water, saw that he was drowning and went to his rescue. She swam with him to shore and saved his life.

  ***The lesson is clear**. If you are going to jump into someone else's turmoil, you must be fully prepared yourself or there can be dire consequences.*

  The story of the seven sons of Secva. Take time to read it in Acts 19:13-16. It is a vivid example of young men who were dabbling in spiritual matters totally unprepared. The results were embarrassing to say the least.

- Lead with your heart

  A most important asset that you must bring to this study is embodied in this story.

  The Girl who was an Avid Reader.

  A young lady who loved to read books made this discovery. For many years she would read several books every month. She would then share with a close friend her reflections and feelings about the books. After finishing one book, she called her friend and explained, "it was kind of dull and uninteresting and I didn't care for it very much". A short time later she met a young man and they started dating. She noticed the young man had the same name as the author of this book. When she questioned him about it he said, "It's no coincidence, I wrote the book." That night she went home and with great enthusiasm reread the book. She called her friend in the morning and told her how very rich and interesting this book was. Her friend responded, "Wait a minute! You told me about this book just two weeks ago. You told me you didn't like it very much and it was kind of dull." The girl responded, "Oh, yes, that's true. I did say that. But that was before I fell in love with the author!"

There is a ***spiritual truth here we cannot miss…***
If we are to get the greatest understanding out of studying God's Word, the Bible, it is most important that we fall in love with the Author. As you study the riches of God's Word you become part of this wonderful family that reaches around the world.

WHAT YOU WILL RECEIVE
CIRCLE THESE THREE KEYS

- **Inheritance**
  Eph 1:11 Because of Christ, we have received an inheritance, for He chose us from the beginning. Part of the great inheritance we have through Christ is the incomparable Word of God. Yet millions of Christians do not yet have these riches or know the depth of their inheritance in the Word. Knowing how to use the Life Application Bible and its many features will enable you to receive this incredible inheritance. Your inheritance is the Word of God. This study is part of the "reading of the will".
- **Spiritual possessions**
  This study will increase your spiritual possessions. It will add to your Scripture resources, footnote insights, riches found in the study guides and other related material.
- **Access to riches**
  You may have money in the bank but unless you have a MAC card (bank card) you cannot access your account and receive cash. You may have knowledge of the vast resources and information found on the internet, but unless you have a computer you have no way to access this information. Through the use of this book and the seminar we have given thousands of Christians access to the riches of the Life Application Bible. In several hours of guided reading and instruction you will find depths of understanding and insights into using the Life Application Bible and its many features that would ordinarily take months or even years to find on your own.

Now we want to give you a concrete example of access. One of the ways you receive access to the riches of the Life Application Bible is through our **ten study guides.**

The following is a portion of the study guide entitled, "Using the Life Application Bible to Share the Wonderful Message Of Salvation in Jesus". It covers seven key topics relating to the subject of salvation.

- The Problem of Sin and God's Answer
- Salvation in Jesus
- We Need to Confess Our Sins
- Repentance
- Justification By Faith
- God's Forgiveness
- Our Guilt is Removed

We are going to look at an example from the topic **Our Guilt is Removed**

POWERFULLY EXPERIENCING THE WORD EXPLAINED THROUGH A FOOTNOTE
The Life Application Bible has had a great impact on people in drug and alcohol recovery programs. They often suffer under the guilt and condemnation of past sins and don't believe they are really forgiven. To break the hold of guilt and condemnation we share the following powerful Scripture and footnote combination.

ROMANS 4:6-8 RIGHT STANDING WITH GOD
King David spoke of this, describing the happiness of an undeserving sinner who is declared to be righteous:
"Oh, what joy for those whose disobedience is forgiven, whose sins are put out of sight. Yes, what joy for those whose sin is no longer counted against them by the Lord."

FOOTNOTE

What can we do to get rid of guilt? King David was guilty of terrible sins—adultery, murder, lying—and yet he experienced the joy of forgiveness. We, too, can have this joy when we (1) quit denying our guilt and recognize that we have sinned, (2) admit our guilt to God and ask for His forgiveness, and (3) let go of our guilt and believe that God has forgiven us. This can be difficult when a sin has taken root in our life over many years, when it is very serious, or when it involves others. We must remember that Jesus is willing and able to forgive every sin. **In view of the tremendous price He paid on the cross, it is arrogant to think that there is any sin too great for Him to forgive.** Even though our faith is weak, our conscience is sensitive, and our memory haunts us, **God's Word declares that sins confessed are sins forgiven (1 John 1:9).**

When this Scripture and footnote is read tremendous things happen. Many times we see tears of joy and relief as guilt is washed away. Burdens are lifted, faces light up. A transformation is experienced. Some record it in their notes so they will never forget. Imagine the power of ministering these kinds of truths to a guilt-ridden person. These life-changing principles can be released in the lives of others if you know where to find the Scriptures and footnotes. **IF YOU HAVE ACCESS.**

The following study guide has been designed to give you tremendous access to key Scriptures that have explanatory footnotes on a variety of subjects that can set people free, change lives, bring people from the kingdom of darkness to Jesus and the Kingdom of Light.

There is power in the study of God's Word to bring recovery, restoration and new beginnings

STUDY GUIDE #1
USING THE LIFE APPLICATION BIBLE TO SHARE THE WONDERFUL MESSAGE OF SALVATION IN JESUS

Many have asked...can you tell us what are some of the best Scripture passages with footnotes from the Life Application Bible, footnotes we can use in understanding God's gift of salvation and in leading others to Christ? Here are some great footnotes and helpful charts.
Our research covers the following subjects:

- **The Problem of Sin and God's Answer**
- **Salvation in Jesus**
- **We Need to Confess Our Sins**
- **Repentance**
- **Justification by Faith**
- **God's Forgiveness**
- **Our Guilt is Removed**

We pray they will inspire you to research the Life Application Bible and add to this list.
Remember to read each Scripture passage first, then ponder and reflect on the passage and the footnote together.
Pray and ask the Holy Spirit to guide you and help you to share the appropriate Scripture passages and footnotes with those you are leading to Christ.

The Problem of Sin and God's Answer

Sin separates us from a holy God bringing judgment and spiritual death. God's perfect sacrifice was needed

- **Romans 6:23 The wages of sin is death**
  Footnote: we must choose between two masters
- **Romans 3:23 All have sinned**
  Footnote: all sin separates us, all can be forgiven
- **Romans 3:24 Redemption through Jesus**
  Footnote: your sin record is wiped clean
- **Psalm 103:11-12 Our sins have been completely removed**
  Footnote: God forgives and forgets. God's love motivated Him to save us

- **John 3:16-17 God so loved the world He gave His Son to save you**
  Three footnotes
  1. A guarantee of eternal life for all believers
  2. You must believe to receive Christ and eternal life
  3. What it means to believe in Jesus

Chart Research ***The Problem Of Sin And God's Answer***

1. **What has God done about sin**
   Located in Rom 6 this chart is an excellent summary of God's action regarding sin. Be sure to read the footnotes related to the passages given
2. **Why did Jesus have to die**
   Located in Mark 15 this chart explains how God dealt with sin.

Salvation in Jesus

- **John 1:12-13 Being reborn**
  Footnote: the spiritual impact of the new birth

Salvation through Christ is dramatically foreshadowed through the Passover lamb

- **Exodus 12:1-27**
  Key footnotes:
  Ex 12:3 the sacrifice of a lamb
  Ex 12:6-11 the protection of the blood
  Ex 12:17, 23 our Passover
- **Acts 4:12 Salvation in Jesus alone**
  Footnote: God designated Jesus Savior of the world
- **Romans 10:8-12 The salvation message condensed**
  Footnote: how to become a Christian
- **Romans 10:13-15 Sent to tell others**
  Footnote: is God calling you to tell others?
- **Mt 7:13-14 The gateway to life is narrow**
  Footnote: the one way to salvation is Jesus
- **Luke 13:22-30 Seek Jesus now**
  Footnote Luke 13:23-24 earnestly desire and diligently follow

- **John 3:5-8 You must be born again**
  Footnote: John 3:8 being born again is a gift of God through the Holy Spirit
- **John 6:68-69 Only One has the words of eternal life**
  Footnote: salvation is a matter of receiving or rejecting Jesus
- **Luke 14:15-24 The privilege of having a share in the kingdom**
  Footnote: do not delay it may be too late
- **John 17:1-5 Jesus the way**
  Footnote: John 17:3 how we get eternal life
- **Eph 2:1-10 saved by Christ's death**
  Footnote: Eph 2:3 without Christ we were dead and lost
  Footnote: Eph 2:4-5 in His mercy and love He brought us to life
  Footnote: Eph 2:6 raised with Christ
  Footnote: Eph 2:8-9 responding to the gift

Chart Research…* Salvation In Jesus*****

1. <u>**Salvation's Freeway**</u>
   This chart is located in Rom 2 and presents a "Roman's road" path of salvation. Be sure to read the footnotes connected with these passages.
2. <u>**From Death to Life**</u>
   Located in Col 3 this chart gives insights into new life in Christ and what to expect

We Need to Confess Our Sins

- **Ps 32:5 We are not to hide our sin**
  Footnote: what is confession?
- **Lev 5:5 Confession is needed**
  Footnote: confessing sin is vital to us
- **2 Sm 12:13 David acknowledged his sin**
  Footnote: confessing clears the way for forgiveness
- **2 Sm 12:20-24 Confessing brings a fresh start**
  Footnote: makes possible a new beginning
- **Prov 28:13 Confess and forsake sins**
  Footnote: we can learn from our mistakes
- **1 John 1:9 If we confess our sins, He is faithful to forgive**
  Footnote: confessing sins, the deeper understanding

For greater understanding
Read Psalm 32 and Psalm 51 and the footnotes; these are considered the penitential psalms.

Chart Research…* We Need To Confess Our Sin*****

<u>Confession, Repentance and Forgiveness</u>

Located between Psalm 32 and Psalm 33 this chart is a great help in understanding God's plan of salvation. The psalmists rejoiced in the knowledge that God would respond to confession and repentance with complete forgiveness. Remember to read the psalms recommended in the chart.

Repentance

- **Luke 3:1-18 John the Baptist calls for repentance**
  <u>Footnote</u>: Luke 3:3 turn away from sin and turn towards God
  <u>Footnote</u>: Luke 3:7 sincere motivations are needed
  <u>Footnote:</u> Luke 3:8-9 confession of sins and a changed life go together
- **Mt. 3:1-2 Repent the kingdom of God is near**
  <u>Footnote</u>: understanding repentance, make a 180 degree turn
- **Mt 3: 4-6 John the Baptist preaches, many respond**
  <u>Footnote</u>: Mt 3:6 what repentance means
- **1 Kgs 21:25-29 The repentance of evil King Ahab**
  <u>Footnote</u>: 1 Kgs 21:29 no one is to evil to repent
- **Neh 9:28-31 Rescued repeatedly**
  <u>Footnote</u>: no limit to the number of times you can repent
- **Ex 9:27-34 Pharaoh lies**
  <u>Footnote:</u> example of false repentance
- **Jonah 3: 6-10 An example of true repentance**
  <u>Footnote</u>: Jonah 3:10 hear God's word, respond with humility not stubbornness
- **Luke 15:8-10 All heaven rejoices when one repents**
  <u>Footnote</u>: repentance of one causes celebration in heaven

Justification by Faith

- **John 20:30-31 Reading the Bible will help you believe**
  Footnote: study the gospels to understand the life and mission of Jesus
- **Romans 3:28 Right standing with God through faith**
  Footnote: four points why God choose salvation through faith
- **John 5:24 Listen to Jesus' message and believe**
  Footnote: accept Jesus as Savior
- **Romans 4:4-5 Saved through faith**
  Footnote: Rom 4:4 it's a free gift
  Footnote: Rom 4:5 it is Jesus who saves
- **Romans 8:12-17 Turn from sin and be led by the Spirit**
  Footnote: 8:14-17 guidance for His children

Chart Research ***Justification By Faith***

1. **Faith**
   Located in Romans 1 this chart provides a good biblical understanding of the term faith.
2. **Salvation through Faith**
   This chart is located in Colossians 2 and explains that Christ is the answer.

God's Forgiveness

- **Heb 9:22 The shedding of blood is needed**
  Footnote: why does forgiveness require the shedding of blood
- **1 Chr 21:8 David admits his sin**
  Footnote: confession & repentance essential to forgiveness
- **2 Chr 7:14 Conditions for forgiveness**
  Footnote: four steps that lead to forgiveness
- **Psalm 51:1-7 Sins blotted out**
  Footnote: no sin too great for God to forgive

God forgives and forgets confessed sin

- **Psalm 130:3-4 God forgives completely**
  Footnote: God keeps no record of our sins
- **Heb 10:17 God will remember our sins no more**
  Footnote: confessed sin forgotten
- **Isaiah 43:25 God doesn't think of our sin again**
  Footnote: does not remind us of our confessed sin

Chart Research…*God's Forgiveness*****

Jesus and forgiveness

Located in Mt.19. In this chart Jesus demonstrates His willingness to forgive. Be sure to read the examples given and related footnotes.

Our Guilt is Removed

- **Rom 3:21-29 Christ took our punishment**
  Footnote: declared not guilty
- **Rom 8:1-17 There is now no condemnation**
  Footnote: Rom 8:1 not guilty, let him go free
  Footnote: Rom 8:3 Jesus paid the penalty
- **Rom 4:6-8 The joy of being forgiven**
  Footnote: how to receive this joy (3 points)
- **Rom 8:33-34 Who dares accuse God's chosen**
  Footnote: Rom 3:34 sin and guilt removed yet Satan accuses
- **Phil 3:13-14 Forgetting what lies behind**
  Footnote: let go of past guilt and look forward

Perhaps you already have ideas about how you could use these salvation riches you now have access to. This page is for your notes and reflections.

Will you let the King's Message flow through you?

In 1930 a man named Harold Vidian was in charge of broadcasting England's King George V's opening address at the London Arms Conference. The king's message was to be sent by radio around the world. A few minutes before the king was to speak one of the CBS news team tripped over an electrical wire and broke it, cutting off the whole American audience. Without hesitation, chief controller, Harold Vidian, grasped one end of the broken wires in his right hand and the other in his left, thus restoring the circuit. Electricity surged through his body. Ignoring the pain, Vidian held on until the king had finished his address.

Will you allow the power of the King's Message to flow through you? It may be difficult, painful and challenging, but the Message of the King of Kings must go out to the whole world. Through human means it will be transmitted as hearts are surrendered and lives yielded to Him.

MORE ACCESS - MORE SAMPLING THE RICHES

The focus of this study is to sample two of the most important features referred to as FOOTNOTES AND CHARTS. A feature is a **study tool, a teaching tool or a reference tool** found in the Life Application Bible. Remember also, this Bible has been called "A Bible College in a book", and "The Teacher's Resource Bible". So we will look at its riches as a source for our personal study and as a resource to teach others.

SAMPLE 1: ROMANS 3:28 (FOOTNOTE)

Suppose on short notice you have been asked to explain to some new believers
"Why God chose justification by faith apart from the Law".

Let's consider Romans 3:28.
So we are made right with God through faith and not by obeying the law.

In the Life Application Bible read the footnote at the bottom of the page and notice it contains a four-point teaching outline that will make it easy to explain this passage.

Romans 3:28 FOOTNOTE: Why does God save us by faith alone?

(1) Faith eliminates the pride of human effort, because faith is not a deed that we do.

(2) Faith exalts what God has done, not what we do.

(3) Faith admits that we can't keep the law or measure up to God's standards—we need help.

(4) Faith is based on our relationship with God, not our performance for God.

This is only one of the 10,000 footnotes in this Bible. Many contain insights that can be used as point-by-point teaching outlines.

Take time to write your thoughts and reflections.

SAMPLE 2: COLOSSIANS 1 (CHART)

Some of the most requested Bible teachings today are those on Prayer. Many have a great desire to pray for others but don't know how to begin.
In Colossians 1 the chart entitled *"How to Pray for Other Christians"* is a great resource.
This chart provides a seven point teaching outline on one aspect of prayer based on Paul's writings in chapter one of Colossians.

"How to Pray for Other Christians"

1. Be thankful for their faith and changed lives (1:3)
2. Ask God to help them know what he wants them to do (1:9)
3. Ask God to give them deep spiritual understanding (1:9)
4. Ask God to help them live for him (1:10)
5. Ask God to give them more knowledge of himself (1:10)
6. Ask God to give them strength for endurance (1:11)
7. Ask God to fill them with joy, strength and thankfulness (1:11)

How many people in your life could be touched if you prayed in this way?

This is another wonderful teaching tool known as CHARTS. The Life Application Bible contains more than 265 charts.

What ideas do you have to use this resource?

Here are two more samples worth remembering and may be of special use to pastors and church leaders.
SAMPLE 3 ----ROMANS 12:6-8 (FOOTNOTE)
God tells us in His Word that each person in the body has gifts for the upbuilding of the church. To use them effectively, in love and harmony, is a challenge. This footnote provides five special insights that, when explained and understood, will bring those in your congregation to a starting point that will help them effectively use their gifts together.

Romans 12:6-8 Just as our bodies have many parts and each part has a special function, so it is with Christ's body. We are all parts of his one body, and each of us has different work to do. And since we are all one body in Christ, we belong to each other, and each of us needs all the others. God has given each of us the ability to do certain things well. So if God has given you the ability to prophesy, speak out when you have faith that God is speaking through you. If your gift is that of serving others, serve them well. If you are a teacher, do a good job of teaching. If your gift is to encourage others, do it! If you have money, share it generously. If God has given you leadership ability, take the responsibility seriously. And if you have a gift for showing kindness to others, do it gladly.

FOOTNOTE God gives us gifts so we can build up his church. To use them effectively, we must (1) realize that all gifts and abilities come from God; (2) understand that not everyone has the same gifts; (3) know who we are and what we do best; (4) dedicate our gifts to God's service and not to our personal success; (5) be willing to utilize our gifts wholeheartedly, not holding back anything from God's service.

SUGGESTED: Some church leaders may want to include these five points in their church bulletin so all in the church can reflect upon them.

SAMPLE 4----LOCATED IN HEBREWS 5 (CHART)

Many pastors have told us one of the greatest needs in their churches is to bring people to maturity. For this they need God's wisdom. The following chart, *"The Choices of Maturity"*, is an excellent tool for pastors who want to call their people to make mature choices. It is also helpful for each person's self-evaluation and personal growth. It is important for church members to see the choices offered as a challenge not as a criticism.

"The Choices of Maturity"
Mature Choices versus Immature Choices

- Teaching others rather than just being taught
- Developing depth of understanding rather than struggling with the basics
- Self-evaluation rather than self-criticism
- Seeking unity rather than promoting disunity
- Desiring spiritual challenges rather than desiring entertainment
- Careful study and observation rather than opinions and halfhearted efforts
- Active faith rather than cautious apathy and doubt
- Confidence rather than fear
- Feelings experienced and evaluated in the light of God's Word rather than experiences evaluated according to feelings

One way to evaluate spiritual maturity is by looking at the choices we make. The writer of Hebrews notes many of the ways these choices change with personal growth.

SAMPLE 5----FAVORITE SCRIPTURE (FOOTNOTE RESEARCH)

Turn in the Life Application Bible to your favorite Scripture and read the related footnote.

What did you discover? Record it here.

This is YOUR PERSONAL EXPERIENCE using the Life Application Bible. Many discover new insights to their favorite passage, which they receive as God speaking to them or revealing His Word to them in a personal way. It is important to take time to share this with others.

In the Life Application Bible a most loved passage, John 3:16, has three footnotes. Read these footnotes and write your reflections. The depths of the personal insights found in these footnotes can be exceptionally enriching and can be used to share with others.

COMBINED CHART AND FOOTNOTE RESEARCH
SEVEN REASONS NOT TO WORRY

We have sampled two of the rich features of the Life Application Bible FOOTNOTES AND CHARTS
The focus of this study is to see how they can be combined together to expand our knowledge of Bible truths and to help us develop teaching and Bible study outlines that can enrich others. We will also take notice of a special section of the Life Application Bible containing a chart and related footnotes on the subject of worry.
Every Christian who has ever experienced the heaviness and hindrance of worry should become familiar with these great insights from God's Word.

Consider being in this situation: the economy is floundering and jobs are in jeopardy. You notice many of your friends are suffering the uncertainties of not knowing how they will earn money and support their families. There seems to be no way out of the situation or a solution to the problem. You recognize that often people are overcome by worry before they even realize it. You look to God's Word for answers. Turn to Matthew 6:25-34; locate the chart *Seven Reasons Not to Worry* found at the end of Matthew 6.

- Choose one or two points that you would share with your friends
- Write them down here
- Explain what they are and why you selected them
- Read the related footnotes and record any you find helpful

EXAMPLE: One person prepared the following teaching outline:

1. **God can be trusted**
   Matthew 6:25 The same God who created life in you can be trusted with the details of your life.
2. **Worrying hinders our work**
   Matthew 6:26 Worrying about the future hampers your efforts for today.
3. **Worrying doesn't help**
   Matthew 6:27 Worrying is more harmful than helpful.
4. **God does hear us**
   Matthew 6:28-30 God does not ignore those who depend on Him.
5. **Worry reveals lack of trust in God**
   Matthew 6:31-32 Worry shows a lack of faith in and understanding of God.
6. **Worry prevents us from pursuing God's work**
   Matthew 6:33 There are real challenges God wants us to pursue, and worrying keeps us from them.
7. **Worrying about tomorrow is time wasted**
   Matthew 6:34 Living one day at a time keeps us from being consumed with worry.

The related footnotes detail even more the ways worry hinders us. They also show how worry interferes with or cripples our efforts to do God's work. The footnotes then give practical ways not only to overcome the present worry but also to avoid worry in the future. **See the footnote on Matthew 6:25 which lists some ill effects of worry.**

*****You can use this example as a pattern for your own point-by-point teaching outline.**

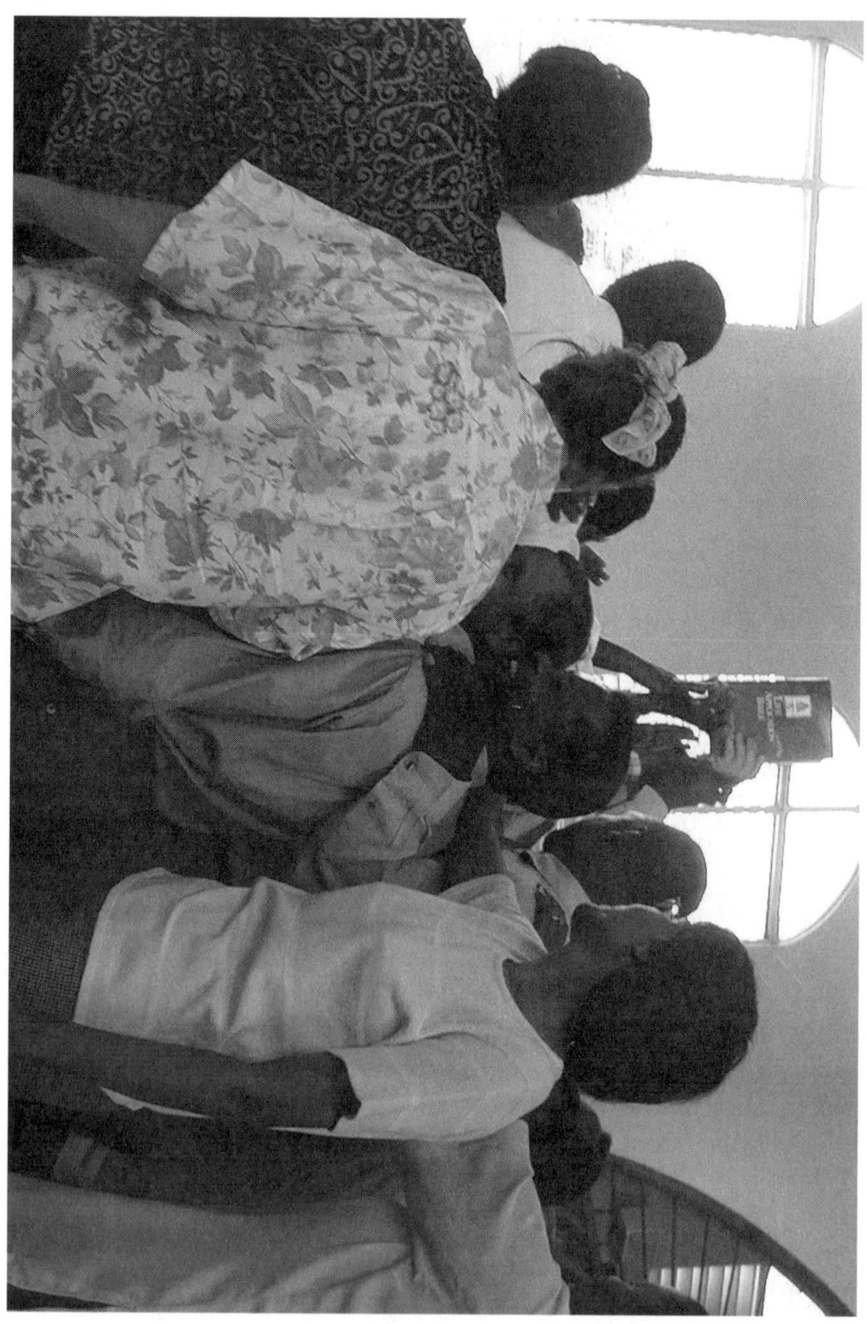

WE DON'T NEED TO WORRY, GOD PROVIDES FOR HIS PEOPLE

We received a request to bring the Life Application Bible Seminar to some pastors and teachers in the Dominican Republic, a beautiful island in the Caribbean. At the time our mission account was low on funds, so we took the whole matter to prayer and asked the Lord for direction. Some of the mission ladies on our team had an idea. It was nearing the Easter season and they thought they could purchase some decorative candles and sell them at a profit to church members. We could use the funds to purchase the five hundred Life Application Bibles we needed. It would be necessary to sell a great number of candles.

I called and asked the vice-president of the publishing house to send us the catalog from the religious goods division to select the candles we wanted.

Being a good Christian man, he told us he would give us the best possible price on our order, a 60% discount. While on the phone he asked for prayer. He had to fly to Europe that week to visit some customers and had an exhausting schedule. That evening as I knelt in prayer the Lord impressed upon my heart to prayer for his safety in the air. When I did the burden lifted. Two weeks passed, the ladies selected the candles from the catalog and I called him to place the order. I mentioned the burden of prayer I had for him regarding his trip to Europe and his safety in the air.

There was a silence on the other end of the phone. Then he started to thank me for the prayer and he told the following story: "We were flying out of O'Hare International Airport in Chicago bound for Europe. The plane was fully loaded with fuel. A lady on the flight became deathly ill and we had to make an emergency landing at a small airport in Nova Scotia. The airport had only a short runway and there was no opportunity to dump the fuel before we landed. As we touched down two tires blew out on one side of the plane. The pilot was so hard on the brake that the landing gear caught on fire. We were at the very end of the runway when the plane finally stopped. The crew quickly evacuated everyone to the far end of the runway, fearing the plane and the fuel would explode. He then said, "Brother Jim, I had a narrow escape. I want to thank you so much for listening to the Lord and praying for me and by the way, the candle order you just placed will be free."

The candles were sold at church and the funds were enough to pay for all the bibles we needed for the pastors in the Dominican Republic. We went to conduct the seminar and shared the story, relating that God, not us, had provided these bibles for them. Great shouts of joy went forth, with praise to God as their provider. That spirit of joy and thanks pervaded the whole seminar. It was a time we will never forget.

STUDY GUIDE #2 ADDITIONAL FOOTNOTE RESEARCH

The focus of this study guide is to help you discover more of the riches in the Life Application Bible. It lists some of the key footnotes found in the Old Testament that contain point-by-point teaching outlines, their location and a short description of each.

There are other footnotes that contain **unnumbered point-by-point teaching outlines.**

An example would be:
Ps 34:1 FF This footnote lists God's blessings and how they are received.

Remember: To receive the deepest insights from these footnotes, it is important to research all of the cross-references given.
We encourage you to create your own footnote list to share and teach from.

The following is our list of some of the best footnotes with outlines found in the Old Testament:

Ex 13:12-14	What does it mean "to redeem every first-born son"? This ritual served three purposes
Lev 1:3	What did animal sacrifice teach people (3 points)
Deut 5:7	Do not worship other gods, put God first (5 points)
Jos 7:1 FF	The results of Achan's sin (5 points) The results of eliminating sin from the community (4 points) also the footnote found in Jos 8:1
1 Sam 1:18	How Hannah overcame discouragement (3 points)
1 Sam 14: 24	Guard against making impulsive oaths (3 points)

1 Sam 18:1-4	The Jonathan and David friendship (4 points)
2 Sam 5:19-25	David followed God's instruction in battle so must we (6 points)
2 Sam 11:1 FF	David falls into sin (7 points)
1 Chron 16:7-38	4 Elements of true thanksgiving (fully expressing your thanks to God)
Est 4:11-5:2	4 point model for approaching a difficult or dangerous task
Ps 18:2-3	God's care characterized with 5 military symbols
Ps 40:1-4	David benefits from waiting for God (4 points)
Ps 106:40-42	When troubles can be helpful (7 insights)
Ps 133:1-3	The importance of unity (3 Insights)
Ps 145:14	God is able to lift us when we are burdened because (11 insights)
Prov 18:13, 15, 17	3 Principles for making sound decisions
Ecclesiastes 1:8-11	5 Commonly asked questions about life. True and lasting meaning to life is found in God alone.
Ecclesiastes 1:16-18	Two kinds of wisdom, choose the wisdom that comes from God
Ecclesiastes 3:11	God has planted eternity in the human heart (3 insights)
Isaiah 3:14	Why is justice so important in the Bible (4 good insights)

Isaiah 41:8-10	God's chosen need not fear (3 reasons)
Jer 2:4-8	Why the prophets recited history to God's people (4 points)
Jer 7:9-11	Parallels between how the people of Judah view their temple and how many today view their churches (3 observations)
Dan 3:15	8 excuses to worship an idol and save your life

As you study the Life Application Bible locate and record your favorite point-by-point teaching outlines found in the New Testament footnotes. Write them on the following page.

CHAPTER ONE REVIEW QUESTIONS - NOTE: The answers to all the above questions can be found in the previous pages.

1. What two features have we covered so far?

   ____

2. How many footnotes are in the Life Application Bible?

   ____

3. How many charts are in the Life Application Bible?

   ____

4. Name a chart we covered in this chapter.

   ____

5. Romans 3:28 has a ______________________________
   in the footnote.

6. How many study guides are included with this course?

   ____

7. The Life Application Bible is known as a

   ____

8. Write down the three keys to understanding what you will receive in this course.

   ____

9. What is the name of the first study guide?

   ____

10. What is the name of the chart in the combined chart and footnote study we did?

    ____

11. What is the definition of a feature?

CHAPTER 2 BECOMING FAMILIAR WITH THE INDEX TO NOTES

The focus of this study is to become familiar with using the valuable resource known as the Index to Notes. This is the key index to the whole Bible and its 10,000 footnotes. It is found after the book of Revelation and is set up like a dictionary. It has hundreds of headings, listing people, subjects and topics in alphabetical order followed by a Scripture reference and a page number. It also includes a list of notes, maps, charts and personality profiles. When you come to realize that all the subjects and topics listed have key Scripture references and great footnotes and that each footnote contains insights, explanation or application of God's Word, your research and study time becomes a joy and a labor of love, a time that you look forward to, a rich banquet feast to savor and enjoy.

In this chapter we will use the Index to Notes, also called the Master Index to learn more about
The Person of the Holy Spirit
The Subject of Repentance
The Person of Jesus

<u>CHAPTER 2</u> BECOMING FAMILIAR WITH THE INDEX TO NOTES

SECTION 1 HOLY SPIRIT RESEARCH

Some of the most requested teachings today are those related to the Holy Spirit. People have a hunger and a desire to know Him and to experience His power and joy in their lives. The focus of this study is to learn more about the Holy Spirit and His work by examining the listing on the Holy Spirit in the Index to Notes. The Life Application Bible provides 63 references, each with a footnote that is both helpful and informative.

Many have shared that learning to use this resource has been an answer to their prayer to grow in knowledge of the Holy Spirit.

<u>Suppose</u> you have been called on to prepare a presentation on the Holy Spirit for your Bible study group. Using the index to notes (found after the Book of Revelation)

- locate the section on the Holy Spirit
- look over the sixty-three references

OPTION 1

- research one reference about the topic of the Holy Spirit
- read any related footnote(s)
- record the Scripture reference you have selected

  ____
- write down your thoughts on this passage and the footnote

  ____
  ____
  ____
  ____

OPTION 2

- select and research three or four references about the Holy Spirit. Write them here:

  ____
  ____
  ____
  ____
  ____
  ____

- read all related footnotes
- write some of your thoughts and reflections here:

  ____
  ____
  ____
  ____
  ____
  ____

COMPLETED EXAMPLE: From the section on the Holy Spirit Jim selected the topic 'The Role and Work of the Holy Spirit in the lives of Believers'. He found in the footnotes of Acts 1:5 the following three point teaching outline:

1. The Holy Spirit marks the beginning of the Christian life Romans 8:9; 1 Corinthians 6:17; Romans 8:14-17; Galatians 4:6-7; 1 Corinthians 12:13.

2. The Holy Spirit is the life changing power in the Christian life Galatians 3:3; Philippians 1:6.

3. The Holy Spirit provides the unity in the Christian life Ephesians 2:19-22; 1 Corinthians 12:11; Ephesians 4:4.

COMMENT: Jim found that the sixty-three references to the Holy Spirit were a great help in locating the topic he wanted to develop as well as providing a source of information from which to draw.

PATTON AND ROMMEL

You might have heard of General George Patton, a famous military leader and tank commander of World War II. His counterpart in the German army was General Erwin Rommel, known as 'the Desert Fox'. These two military leaders were to encounter each other in North Africa. During a battle when Patton's troops and tanks were engaged in a successful counter-attack against Rommel's forces, Patton, realizing he had the victory, shouted out in the thick of battle, "I read your book, Rommel, I read your book!" And that he did. Rommel had written a book, "Infantry Attacks". In it he carefully detailed his military strategy. Patton, having read the book and knowing what to expect, planned his strategic moves and was able to win the victory. ***There is a parallel here in the spiritual world****. Satan, our enemy, has never authored a book, but his purpose is well documented and exposed in God's Word. If we understand Satan's plans and tactics, we will be forewarned and prepared and he will never defeat us in battle. Indeed, the Word of God says in 2 Corinthians 2:11 (KJV) Satan should not get an advantage over us for we are not ignorant of his devices.*

STUDY GUIDE #3 USING THE LIFE APPLICATION BIBLE AS A RESEARCH TOOL

The focus of this study guide is to provide an example of how the Life Application Bible can be used to research a specific subject. It also provides a sampling of some of the Scripture and footnote information found in the Life Application Bible on the subject of the occult and occult practices. We felt it is important to share this information because as we travel teaching others to use the Life Application Bible we encounter occult practices around the world. Some of us may even have friends, neighbors and relatives involved in these practices. As you study the following, let God's Word reveal to you His will in these matters.

Some occult practices would be:

Different forms of witchcraft, sorcery, casting spells, preparing potions, fortune telling, tarot cards, reading tea leaves, ouija board, crystal balls, psychic readings, horoscopes, séances, contacting the dead.
People get involved with these practices for some of the following reasons:

Many are simply curious
Others are seeking guidance or want to know the future
Some are seeking power and recognition
Many want to be entertained or do it for fun
Some devious people desire to make money using occult practices like the owners of the slave girl (Acts 16:16-18)

There are many who believe it is OK to be involved with the occult, but the ultimate authority on the subject is God and His Word.
The following selections of Scripture from the Life Application Bible and accompanying footnotes can be helpful in beginning your research to learn the truth about occult practices.

What does God say about these practices? He forbids it
Deut 18:10-11 Let no one be found among you who sacrifices his son or daughter in the fire, who practices divination or sorcery, interprets omens, engages in witchcraft, or casts spells, or who is a medium or spiritist or who consults the dead.

Life App footnote: Deut 18:10 Child sacrifice and occult practices were strictly forbidden by God. These practices were common among pagan religions. Israel's own neighbors actually sacrificed their children to the god Molech (Lev 20:2-5) Other neighboring religions used supernatural means, such as contacting the spirit world, to foretell the future and gain guidance. Because of these wicked practices God would drive out the pagan nations (18:12). The Israelites were to replace their evil practices with the worship of the one true God.

Life Application footnote: Deut 18:10-13 The Israelites were naturally curious about the occult practices of the Canaanite religions. But Satan is behind the occult, and God flatly forbade Israel to have anything to do with it. Today people are still fascinated by horoscopes, fortune telling, witchcraft and bizarre cults. Often their interest comes from a desire to know and control the future. But Satan is no less dangerous today than he was in Moses' time. In the Bible, God tells us all we need to know about what is going to happen. The information Satan offers is likely to be distorted or completely false. With the trustworthy guidance of the Holy Spirit through the Bible and the church, we don't need to turn to occult sources for faulty information. WAIT A MINUTE…Psychics and mediums help police solve crimes. How can what they do be bad? How can it be wrong to go to them if what they say is true?

Acts 16:16-18 Once when we were going to the place of prayer, we were met by a slave girl who had a spirit by which she predicted the future. She earned a great deal of money for her owners by fortune telling. This girl followed Paul and the rest of us shouting, "These men are servants of the Most High God, who are telling you the way to be saved." She kept this up for many days. Finally Paul became so troubled that he turned around and said to the spirit, "In the Name of Jesus Christ I command you to come out of her!" At that moment the spirit left her.

How can that be wrong?
Life App Bible footnote Acts 16:16 This girl's fortune telling ability came from evil spirits. Fortune telling was a common practice in Greek and Roman culture. There were many superstitious methods by which people thought they could foretell future events, from interpreting omens in nature to communicating with the spirits of the dead. This

young slave girl had an evil spirit and she made her master rich by interpreting signs and telling people their fortunes. Her master was exploiting her unfortunate condition for personal gain.
Life App footnote Acts 16:17-18 What the slave girl said was true, although the source of her knowledge was a demon. Why did a demon announce the truth about Paul, and why did this annoy Paul? If Paul accepted the demon's words he would appear to be linking the gospel with the demon-related activities. This would damage his message about Christ. Truth and evil do not mix.

Today in our time fortune tellers and psychics try to link their powers with Christ and the gospel. To gain credibility they attend church, wear crosses and medals of the saints. They adorn their houses and properties with religious pictures, icons and statues. But the source is still corrupt and can defile you and lead you away from God.
Do you think people are taken in and deceived by psychics and fortunetellers?

2 Thes 2:9 the coming of the lawless one will be in accordance with the work of Satan displayed in all kinds of counterfeit miracles, signs and wonders and in every sort of evil that deceives those who are perishing.

Life App footnote This lawless one will use "counterfeit miracles, signs and wonders" to deceive and draw a following. Miracles from God can help strengthen our faith and lead people to Christ, but all miracles are not necessarily from God. Christ's miracles were significant not just because of their power, but because of their purpose—to help, to heal, and to point us to God. The man of lawlessness will have power to do amazing things, but his power will be from Satan. He will use this power to destroy and to lead people away from God and towards himself. If any so-called religious personality draws attention only to himself or herself, his or her work is not from God.

DON'T BE FOOLED
People involved in occult practices will definitely be able to perform signs and wonders and counterfeit miracles. They will say some things, which are true, but ultimately they and their source will be revealed by studying the Scriptures and following the guidance of the Holy Spirit.

Lev 20:6 Should anyone turn to mediums and fortunetellers and follow their wanton ways, I will turn against such a one and cut him off from his people.

Life App footnote Everyone is interested in what the future holds, and often we look to others for guidance. But God warned about looking to the occult for advice. Mediums and spiritists were outlawed because God was not the source of their information. At best, occult practitioners are fakes whose predictions cannot be trusted. At worst, they are in contact with evil spirit and thus extremely dangerous. We don't need to look at the occult for information about the future. God has given us the Bible so that we may obtain all the information we need---and the Bible's teaching is trustworthy.

The above passages and footnotes are only a sample of the insights available to you using the Life Application Bible. Be sure to research all related Scripture references in the footnotes as well as any cross-reference passages given. Use the Index to Notes and the Dictionary Concordance in the back of the Bible to research parallel or related words and subjects.

As you study take time to research a favorite subject or topic, record your research and use it to help others learn the great truths of God's Word.

Reflecting on the previous study guide information
Write down some of your thoughts and insights.
How can you use this knowledge in everyday life?
What situations can you address now that you are aware of the enemy's tactics?
What preparation can you make to apply this wisdom from God's Word?

CHAPTER 2 BECOMING FAMILIAR WITH THE INDEX TO NOTES

SECTION 2 REPENTANCE

The focus of this study is to help you become familiar with using the Index to Notes as well as exploring a rich special features listing on repentance. People in every generation, especially new believers, need to have a biblical understanding of true repentance. It is key to being set free from the guilt and bondage of sin. This listing can be extremely helpful in pastoral and teaching situations. It is strongly suggested that you read and research all twenty-nine references for your personal enrichment and to share with others.

Suppose you have been called on to present a talk on repentance to new believers. Using the INDEX TO NOTES (found after the book of Revelation)

- Locate the section on Repentance
- Review the twenty-nine references

OPTION 1

- Select 2 references that you consider to be the most important
- Write them here

____

____

____

- Research the ones you have chosen by reading the Scripture
  and the related footnotes
- Write your reflections and thoughts here

____

____

____

____

____

____

OPTION 2

- Write down 4 or 5 points that you would include in your teaching outline

- Research the ones you have chosen by reading the Scripture and the related footnotes

- Explain why you selected them, including some of your own reflections and comments

<u>CHAPTER 2</u> BECOMING FAMILIAR WITH THE INDEX TO NOTES

SECTION 2A REPENTANCE

EXAMPLE: One pastor selected 7 topics and the related footnotes as the basis for his teaching outline.

1. **What repentance means...**
   from the baptism of John --Matthew 3 especially Matthew 3:6 and footnote
2. **True repentance is revealed by changed actions...**
   contrasted by the false repentance of Pharaoh Exodus 9:27-34 and footnote
3. **No one is too evil to repent...**
   illustrated by the repentance of evil King Ahab 1 Kings 21:25-29 and footnote
4. **There is no limit to the number of times you can repent...**seen in God's gracious forgiveness of His people, Israel, after their continual disobedience to His command Nehemiah 9:28-31 and footnote
5. **Repentance is needed for entrance into God's Kingdom...**
   Nicodemus you must be born again John 3 especially John 3:3 and footnote
6. **Repentance is accompanied by humility rather than stubbornness...**
   Nineveh repentance verses Israel's stubbornness Jonah 3 especially verse 10 and footnote
7. **Repentance brings rejoicing in the presence of God and His angels...**
   Luke 15:8-10 and footnote

To this he added his own personal comments and reflections to enrich his presentation. The above completed outline can be used as a pattern for to create teaching outlines on other subjects and topics.

CHAPTER 2 BECOMING FAMILIAR WITH THE INDEX TO NOTES

SECTION 3 LEARNING ABOUT JESUS

The focus of this study is to help you become familiar with using the Index to Notes. You will also discover that the Index to Notes is another way of accessing information about maps and charts. This is a rich resource useful in studying and teaching about the life and ministry of Jesus.

Learning about Jesus is a vital part of having a relationship with Him and growing as a Christian. There isn't any information about His life or ministry that is ever insignificant. To those who love Him, the smallest detail about His life is important and a joy to discover.

This study is divided into three segments covering footnotes, charts and maps.

1. Turn to the Index to Notes in your Life Application Bible
2. Locate the Heading "Jesus Christ"
3. Take time to review the list of 195 footnotes
4. At the end of the list of footnotes notice a list of 35 maps followed by a list of 33 charts

Footnote research

a. Select one of your favorite subjects or events in the life of Jesus
   Record what you selected

   ____

b. Read Scripture and the related footnote
c. Write down any insights or reflections you have gained from your research

   ____

   ____

Chart research

a. Select one of the 33 charts about Jesus that you consider most interesting
Record your choice

____

b. Read through the chart and any related Scripture and footnotes

c. Write down how you found it interesting and share any insights you felt were worth remembering

____
____
____
____

Map research

Often maps help us visualize the life and ministry of Jesus and understand it in new ways

a. Select one of the 35 maps listed for your study and reflection List it here

____

b. Read the caption and observe the format

c. Did you gain any new perspective or understanding about the life and ministry of Jesus? Record it here

____
____
____
____
____

CHAPTER 2 BECOMING FAMILIAR WITH THE INDEX TO NOTES

SECTION 3 LEARNING ABOUT JESUS

Footnote research
COMPLETED EXAMPLE:
Pat chose 'The significance of Jesus' resurrection', Matthew 28:6 for her research.
From the footnote she learned Jesus' resurrection is the key to the Christian faith because:

1. Just as He promised, Jesus rose from the dead. We can be confident, therefore, that He will accomplish all that He has promised.
2. Jesus' bodily resurrection shows us that the living Christ is ruler of God's eternal kingdom, not a false prophet or impostor.
3. We can be certain of our resurrection because He was resurrected. Death is not the end--there is future life.
4. The power that brought Jesus back to life is available to us to bring our spiritually dead selves back to life.
5. The resurrection is the basis for the Church's witness to the world.
   Jesus is more that just a human leader, He is the Son of God.

Chart research
COMPLETED EXAMPLE: Joe chose the chart entitled "What Jesus Said About Love" found in Mark 12. He was impressed by the extensiveness of the chart and the great importance that Jesus placed on love. From the listing Joe chose the heading "Jesus' love extends to each individual". He read the footnote on Mark 10:21 and felt it was worth remembering. Genuine love is able to give tough advice. It doesn't hedge around the truth. Jesus loved us enough to die for us and He also

loved us enough to talk straight to us. If His love were superficial, He would give us only His approval; but because His love is complete, he gives us life-changing challenges.

Map research

COMPLETED EXAMPLE: Jim chose the map depicting Jesus' ministry in Phoenicia, located in Matthew 15. He noticed the great distances and rough terrain Jesus had to travel and the obvious hardships involved in such journeys. Jim noted that Jesus was already living out Romans 12:1 by delivering His body a living sacrifice, holy and pleasing to God, a spiritual act of worship. Even before He went to the cross, Jesus' submission to His Father's plan and the laying down of His life for His sheep was part of His everyday life and should be for each of us.

THE PASTOR'S PLEA SIERRA LEONE SEMINAR WEST AFRICA

"Please Brother Jim, help us learn more about Jesus from this Bible. Our people have a hunger to know Him and we have only limited understanding to give them." This was a request that stirred and touched our hearts. Ten years have passed and the power of the moment and the hunger of the people still resonates within us.

The following study material, gathered specifically to be used with the Life Application Bible, is the result of that heart's cry to know more about Jesus. The **Jesus Study Guide** is dedicated to our wonderful Christian brothers and sisters of Sierra Leone, West Africa. In adversity and trial, they stand as champions for Jesus Christ, proclaiming His Gospel and building His Kingdom.

STUDY GUIDE # 4 JESUS STUDY GUIDE

UNDERSTANDING MORE ABOUT JESUS THROUGH HIS NAMES, HIS TITLES, HIS PRAYERS, HIS PRIESTHOOD, MESSIANIC PROPHECIES AND THEIR FULFILLMENT, AND JESUS STUDY CHARTS

The following study guide is an excellent resource tool for improving our perception and knowledge of the Lord through His names. Studying His Names also helps to enhance and deepen our personal relationship with Him.

The Names of the Lord reveal:

- The Person of God—revealing who He is
- The Power of God—revealing what He is able to do
- The Plan of God—revealing what He desires to do
- The Promise of God—revealing what we can trust Him to do

***NOTE: The designation FN after a name or title indicates a supporting footnote that gives further insight into this name of the Lord.

A. HIS NAMES AND TITLES

Adam 1 Cor 15:45 **FN**

Advocate 1 John 2:1 **FN**

Almighty Rev 1:8
Alpha and Omega Rev 1:8 **FN**
Amen Rev 3:14
Angel Gen 48:16; Ex 23:20-21
Angel of His Presence Isa 63:9
Anointed Psa 2:2
Apostle Heb 3:1 **FN**
Arm of the Lord Isa 51:9-10
Author and Finisher of Our Faith Heb 12:2
Beginning & End of Creation of God Rev 3:14; Rev 22:13
Beloved Eph 1:6
Bishop 1 Pet 2:25
Blessed and Only Potentate 1 Tim 6:15
Branch Jer 23:5 **FN**; Zech 3:8 **FN**
Bread of Life John 6:48
Bridegroom Matt 9:15
Bright and Morning Star Rev 22:16 **FN**
Brightness of the Father's Glory Heb 1:3
Captain of the Lord's Host Josh 5:14
Captain of Salvation Heb 2:10
Carpenter Mark 6:3 **FN**
Carpenter's Son Matt 13:55 **FN**
Chief Shepherd 1 Pet 5:4 **FN**
Chief Cornerstone 1 Pet 2:6 **FN**
Chiefest Among Ten Thousand Song 5:10
Child Isa 9:6; Luke 2:27; Luke 2:43
Chosen of God 1 Pet 2:4
Christ Matt 1:16 **FN**; Luke 9:20
The Christ Matt 16:20 **FN**; Mark 14:61 **FN**
Christ, a King Luke 23:2
Christ Jesus Acts 19:4; Rom 3:24; Rom 8:1; 1 Cor 1:2; 1 Cor 1:30; Heb 3:1; 1 Pet 5:10; 1 Pet 5:14
Christ Jesus Our Lord 1 Tim 1:12; Rom 8:39
Christ of God Luke 9:20
Christ, the chosen of God Luke 23:35
Christ, the Lord Luke 2:11 **FN**
Christ, the Power of God 1 Cor 1:24 **FN**
Christ, the Wisdom of God 1 Cor 1:24 **FN**
Christ, the Son of God Acts 9:20
Christ, Son of the Blessed Mark 14:61
Commander Isa 55:4
Consolation of Israel Luke 2:25
Cornerstone Eph 2:20
Counselor Isa 9:6 **FN**

Covenant of the People Isa 42:6 **FN**
David Jer 30:9
Daysman Job 9:33
Dayspring Luke 1:78
Day Star 2 Pet 1:19
Deliverer Rom 11:26
Desire of All Nations Hag 2:7
Door John 10:7 **FN**
Elect Isa 42:1 **FN**
Emmanuel Isa 7:14
Ensign Isa 11:10
Eternal life 1 John 5:20
Everlasting Father Isa 9:6
Faithful and True Rev 19:11 **FN**
Faithful Witness Rev 1:5 **FN**
Faithful and True Witness Rev 3:14
Finisher of Faith Heb 12:2
First and Last Rev 1:17 **FN**; Rev 2:8; Rev 22:13
First Begotten Heb 1:6 **FN**
First Begotten of the Dead Rev 1:5 **FN**
Firstborn Psa 89:27
Foundation Isa 28:16 **FN**
Fountain Zech 13:1 **FN**
Forerunner Heb 6:20 **FN**
Friend of Sinners Matt 11:19
Gift of God John 4:10
Glory of Israel Luke 2:32
God John 1:1 **FN**
God Blessed Forever Rom 9:5
God Manifest in the Flesh 1 Tim 3:16 **FN**
God of Israel, the Savior Isa 45:15
God of the Whole Earth Isa 54:5
God our Savior 1 Tim 2:3
God's Dear Son Col 1:13
God With Us Matt 1:23 **FN**
Good Master Matt 19:16
Governor Matt 2:6
Great Shepherd of the Sheep Heb 13:20
Head of the Church Eph 5:23
Heir of all Things Heb 1:2 **FN**
High Priest Heb 4:14
Head of Every Man 1 Cor 11:3
Head of the Church Col 1:18 **FN**

Head of the Corner Matt 21:42 **FN**
Holy Child Jesus Acts 4:30
Holy One Psa 16:10; Acts 3:14
Holy One of God Mark 1:24
Holy One of Israel Isa 41:14; Isa 54:5
Holy Thing Luke 1:35 **FN**
Hope (Our) 1 Tim 1:1
Horn of Salvation Luke 1:69
I Am John 8:58 **FN**
Image of God Heb 1:3 **FN**
Israel Isa 49:3
Jehovah Isa 40:3
Jehovah's Fellow Zech 13:7
Jesus Matt 1:21 **FN**
Jesus Christ Matt 1:1 **FN**; John 1:17; John 17:3; Acts 2:38; Acts 4:10; Acts 9:34; Acts 10:36; Acts 16:18; Rom 1:1; Rom 1:3 **FN**; Rom 1:6; Rom 2:16; Rom 5:15; Rom 5:17; Rom 6:3; 1 Cor 1:1; 1 Cor 1:4; 1 Cor 2:2; 2 Cor 1:19 **FN**; 2 Cor 4:6; 2 Cor 13:5; Gal 2:16; Phil 1:8; Phil 2:11; 1 Tim 1:15; Heb 13:8 **FN**; 1 John 1:7; 1 John 2:1
Jesus Christ Our Lord Rom 1:3 **FN**; Rom 6:11; Rom 6:23; 1 Cor 1:9; 1 Cor 7:25
Jesus Christ Our Savior Tit 3:6 **FN**
Jesus of Nazareth Mark 1:24; Luke 24:19
Jesus of Nazareth, King of the Jews John 19:19 **FN**
Jesus, the King of the Jews Matt 27:37
Jesus, the Son of God Heb 4:14 **FN**
Jesus, the Son of Joseph John 6:42
Judge Acts 10:42
Just Man Matt 27:19
Just One Acts 3:14; Acts 7:52; Acts 22:14
Just Person Matt 27:24
King Matt 21:5
King of Israel John 1:49
King of the Jews Matt 2:2
King of Saints Rev 15:3
King of Kings 1 Tim 6:15; Rev 17:14
King of Glory Psa 24:7-10 **FN**
King of Zion Matt 21:5
King over All The Earth Zech 14:9
Lamb Rev 5:6; Rev 5:8; Rev 6:16; Rev 7:9-10; Rev 7:17; Rev 12:11 **FN**; Rev 13:8; Rev 13:11; Rev 14:1; Rev 14:4; Rev 15:3; Rev 17:14; Rev 19:7; Rev 19:9; Rev 21:9; Rev 21:14; Rev 21:22-23; Rev 21:27
Lamb of God John 1:29 **FN**
Lawgiver Isa 33:22

Leader Isa 55:4
Life John 14:6 **FN**
Light John 8:12 **FN**
Light, Everlasting Isa 60:20
Light of he World John 8:12 **FN**
Light to the Gentiles Isa 42:6 **FN**
Light, True John 1:9
Living Bread John 6:51 **FN**
Living Stone 1 Pet 2:4 **FN**
Lion of the Tribe of Judah Rev 5:5 **FN**
Lord Rom 1:3 **FN**
Lord of Lords Rev 17:14; Rev 19:16 **FN**
Lord of All Acts 10:36
Lord our Righteousness Jer 23:6 **FN**
Lord God Almighty Rev 15:3
Lord from Heaven 1 Cor 15:47
Lord and Savior, Jesus Christ 2 Pet 1:11; 2 Pet 3:18
Lord Christ Col 3:24
Lord Jesus Acts 7:59; Col 3:17; 1 Thess 4:12
Lord Jesus Christ Acts 11:17; Acts 16:31; Acts 20:21; Rom 5:1; Rom 5:11; Rom 13:14
Lord Jesus Christ, Our Savior Tit 1:4
Lord of Glory Jam 2:1
Lord of Hosts Isa 44:6
Lord, Mighty in Battle Psa 24:8 **FN**
Lord of the Dead and Living Rom 14:9
Lord of the Sabbath Mark 2:28
Lord Over All Rom 10:12
Lord's Christ Luke 2:26
Lord Strong and Mighty Psa 24:8 **FN**
Lord, The, Our Righteousness Jer 23:6 **FN**
Lord, Your Holy One Isa 43:15
Lord, Your Redeemer Isa 43:14
Man Christ Jesus 1 Tim 2:5 **FN**
Man of Sorrows Isa 53:3 **FN**
Master Matt 23:8
Mediator 1 Tim 2:5 **FN**
Messenger of the Covenant Mal 3:1 **FN**
Messiah John 1:41
Messiah the Prince Dan 9:25
Mighty God Isa 9:6 **FN**
Mighty one of Israel Isa 30:29
Mighty one of Jacob Isa 49:26

Mighty to Save Isa 63:1
Minister of the Sanctuary Heb 8:2
Morning Star Rev 22:16 **FN**
Most Holy Dan 9:24
Most Mighty Psa 45:3
Nazarene Matt 2:23
Offspring of David Rev 22:16 **FN**
Only Begotten John 1:14 **FN**
Only Begotten of the Father John 1:14
Only Begotten Son John 1:18
Only Wise God, Our Savior Jude 1:25
Passover 1 Cor 5:7 **FN**
Plant of Renown Ezek 34:29
Potentate 1 Tim 6:15
Power of God 1 Cor 1:24 **FN**
Physician Matt 9:12
Precious Cornerstone Isa 28:16 **FN**
Priest Heb 7:17 **FN**
Prince Acts 5:31
Prince of Life Acts 3:15 **FN**
Prince of Peace Isa 9:6 **FN**
Prince of the Kings of the Earth Rev 1:5 **FN**
Prophet Deut 18:15 **FN**; Deut 18:18; Matt 21:11; Luke 24:19
Propitiation 1 John 2:2 **FN**
Rabbi John 1:49
Rabboni John 20:16
Ransom 1 Tim 2:6 **FN**
Redeemer Isa 59:20
Resurrection and Life John 11:25 **FN**
Redemption 1 Cor 1:30 **FN**
Righteous Branch Jer 23:5 **FN**
Righteous Judge 2 Tim 4:8 **FN**
Righteous Servant Isa 53:11 **FN**
Righteousness 1 Cor 1:30 **FN**
Rock 1 Cor 10:4
Rock of Offence 1 Pet 2:8 **FN**
Root of David Rev 5:5; Rev 22:16 **FN**
Root of Jesse Isa 11:10
Rose of Sharon Song 2:1
Ruler in Israel Mic 5:2 **FN**
Salvation Luke 2:30
Sanctification 1 Cor 1:30

Sanctuary Isa 8:14
Savior Luke 2:11 **FN**
Savior, Jesus Christ 2 Tim 1:10; Tit 2:13; 2 Pet 1:1
Savior of the Body Eph 5:23
Savior of the World 1 John 4:14
Scepter Num 24:17
Second Man 1 Cor 15:47
Seed of David 2 Tim 2:8 **FN**
Seed of the Woman Gen 3:15
Servant Isa 42:1 **FN**
Servant of Rulers Isa 49:7
Shepherd Mark 14:27
Shepherd and Bishop of Souls 1 Pet 2:25
Shepherd, Chief 1 Pet 5:4 **FN**
Shepherd, Good John 10:11 **FN**
Shepherd, Great Heb 13:20
Shepherd of Israel Psa 80:1
Shiloh Gen 49:10 **FN**
Son of the Father 2 John 1:3
Son of God *See JESUS, THE CHRIST, SON OF GOD*
Son of Man *See JESUS, THE CHRIST, SON OF MAN*
Son of the Blessed Mark 14:61
Son of the Highest Luke 1:32 **FN**
Son of David Matt 9:27 **FN**
Star Num 24:17
Sun of Righteousness Mal 4:2
Surety Heb 7:22
Stone Matt 21:42 **FN**
Stone of Stumbling 1 Pet 2:8 **FN**
Sure Foundation Isa 28:16 **FN**
Teacher John 3:2
True God 1 John 5:20
True Vine John 15:1 **FN**
Truth John 14:6 **FN**
Unspeakable Gift 2 Cor 9:15
Very Christ Acts 9:22
Vine John 15:1 **FN**
Way John 14:6 **FN**
Which Is, Which Was, Which Is To Come Rev 1:4 **FN**
Wisdom Prov 8:12
Wisdom of God 1 Cor 1:24 **FN**
Witness Isa 55:4; Rev 1:5 **FN**
Wonderful Isa 9:6 **FN**

Word John 1:1 **FN**

Word of God Rev 19:13 **FN**

Word of Life 1 John 1:1 **FN**

B. HIS PRAYERS

In a mountain—Matt 14:23; Mark 6:46; Luke 6:12; Luke 9:28
In Gethsemane—Matt 26:36; Mark 14:32; Luke 22:45
The Lord's prayer—Matt 6:9; Luke 11:1
Before day—Mark 1:35
In distress—John 12:27; Heb 5:7
In the wilderness—Luke 5:16
In behalf of Peter—Luke 22:31-32
For the Comforter—John 14:16
After the supper—John 17

C. HIS PRIESTHOOD

Appointed and called by God—Heb 3:1-2; Heb 5:4-5
After the order of Melchizedek—Psa 110:4; Heb 5:6; Heb 6:20; Heb 7:15; Heb 7:17
Superior to Aaron and the Levitical priests—Heb 7:11; Heb 7:16;Heb 7:22; Heb 8:1-2; Heb 8:6
Consecrated with an oath—Heb 7:20-21
Has an unchangeable priesthood—Heb 7:23; Heb 7:28
Is of unblemished purity—Heb 7:26; Heb 7:28
Is faithful—Heb 3:2
Needed no sacrifice for Himself—Heb 7:27
Offered Himself a sacrifice—Heb 9:14; Heb 9:26
His sacrifice superior to all others—Heb 9:13-14; Heb 9:23
Offered sacrifice but once—Heb 7:27
Made reconciliation—Heb 2:17
Obtained redemption for us—Heb 9:12
Entered into heaven—Heb 4:14; Heb 10:12
Sympathizes with saints—Heb 2:18; Heb 4:15
Intercedes—Heb 7:25; Heb 9:24
Blesses—Num 6:23-26; Acts 3:26
On His throne—Zech 6:13
Appointment of, an encouragement to steadfastness—Heb 4:14
Typified:
- **Melchizedek**—Gen 14:18-20
- **Aaron and his sons**—Ex 40:12-15

D. PROPHECIES & FULFILLMENT CONCERNING THE MESSIAH:

Gen. 12:3, "And I will bless them that bless thee..." Gen 18:18; Gen 22:18; Acts 3:25; Gal 3:8
Gen. 17:7, "And I will establish my covenant..." Gen 17:19; Gen 22:16-17; Luke 1:55;Luke 1:72-74
Deut. 18:18, "I will raise them up a Prophet..." Deut 18:18; Acts 3:22-23

Psa. 2:1, "Why do the heathen rage..." Acts 4:25-26
Psa. 2:7, "Thou art my Son..." Acts 13:33; Heb 1:5; Heb
Psa. 8:2, "Out of the mouth of babes and sucklings..." Matt 21:16
Psa. 8:4, "What is man, that thou are mindful of him..." Heb 2:6-8
Psa. 16:8, "I have set the LORD always before me..." Acts 2:25-28; Acts 2:31
Psa. 16:10, "Neither wilt thou suffer thine Holy One..." Acts 13:35
Psa. 22:1, "My God, my God, why hast thou forsaken me?" Matt 27:46; Mark 15:34
Psa. 22:18, "They part my garments among them..." Matt 27:35; Mark 15:24; Luke 23:34; John 19:24
Psa. 22:22, "I will declare thy name unto my brethren..." Heb 2:12
Psa. 31:5, "Into thine hand I commit my spirit..." Luke 23:46
Psa. 41:9, "...hath lifted up his heel against me." John 13:18;Acts 1:16
Psa. 45:6, "Thy throne, O God, is for ever and ever..." Heb 1:8-9
Psa. 68:18, "Thou hast ascended on high..." Eph 4:8-10
Psa. 69:21, "...and in my thirst they gave me vinegar..." Matt 27:48; Mark 15:36; Luke 23:36; John 19:28-29
Psa. 69:25, "Let their habitation be desolate..." Psa 109:8; Acts 1:20
Psa. 95:7, "To day if ye will hear his voice..." Heb 3:7-11; Heb 4:3; Heb 4:5-7
Psa. 102:25, "Of old hast thou laid the foundation..." Heb 1:10-12
Psa. 110:1, "...until I make thine enemies thy footstool." Matt 22:44; Mark 12:36; Luke 20:42; Acts 2:34-35; Heb 1:13
Psa. 110:4, "Thou art a priest for ever..." Heb 5:6
Psa. 118:22, "The stone which the builders refused..." Matt 21:42; Mark 12:10-11; Luke 20:17; Acts 4:11
Psa. 118:26, "Blessed be he that cometh in the name..." Matt 21:9;Mark 11:9; John 12:13
Psa. 132:17, "There will I make the horn of David..." Psa 132:11; Luke 1:69; Acts 2:30
Psa. 7:14, "Behold, a virgin shall conceive..." Matt 1:23
Isa. 9:2, "The people that walked in darkness have seen..." Matt 4:15-16
Isa. 9:7, "Of the increase of his government..." Dan 7:14; Dan 7:27; Luke 1:32-33
Isa. 11:10, "...there shall be a root of Jesse..." Rom 15:12
Isa. 25:8, "He will swallow up death in victory..." 1 Cor 15:54
Isa. 28:16, "I lay in Zion for a foundation a stone..." Rom 9:33; 1 Pet 2:6
Isa. 40:3-5, "The voice of him that crieth in the wilderness..." Matt 3:3; Mark 1:3; Luke 3:4-6
Isa. 42:1-4, "Behold my servant, whom I uphold..." Matt 12:17-21
Isa. 49:6, "I will also give thee for a light to the Gentiles..." Luke 2:32; Acts 13:47-48; Acts 26:23
Isa. 53:1, "Who hath believed our report..." John 12:38; Rom 10:16
Isa. 53:3-6, "He is despised and rejected of men..." Acts 26:22-23
Isa. 53:4-6, "Surely he hath borne our griefs..." Isa 53:11; 1 Pet 2:24-25; Matt 8:17
Isa. 53:9, "...neither was any deceit in his mouth." 1 Pet 2:22
Isa. 53:12, "...and he was numbered with the transgressors." Mark 15:28;Luke 22:37

Isa. 54:13, "And all thy children shall be taught..." John 6:45
Isa. 55:3, "...even the sure mercies of David." Acts 13:34
Isa. 59:20-21, "And the Redeemer shall come to Zion..." Rom 11:26-27
Jer. 31:31-34, "...I will make a new covenant..." Heb 8:8-12; Heb 10:16-17
Hos. 1:10, "...Ye are the sons of the living God." Rom 9:26
Hos. 2:23, "...Thou art my people..." Rom 9:25; 1 Pet 2:10
Joel 2:28, "I will pour out my spirit upon all flesh..." Acts 2:16-21
Amos 9:11-12, "In that day will I raise up the tabernacle..." Acts 15:16-17
Mic. 5:2, "But thou, Bethlehem Ephratah..." Matt 2:5-6; John 7:42
Hab. 1:5, "Behold ye among the heathen, and regard..." Acts 13:40-41
Hag. 2:6, "Yet once ... and I will shake the heavens..." Heb 12:26
Zech. 9:9, "...behold, thy King cometh unto thee..." Matt 21:4-5; John 12:14-15
Zech. 11:13, "Cast it unto the potter..." Matt 27:9-10
Zech. 12:10, "...look upon me whom they have pierced..." John 19:37
Zech. 13:7, "...smite the shepherd..." Matt 26:31; Matt 26:56; Mark 14:27; Mark 14:50
Mal. 3:1, "Behold, I will send my messenger..." Matt 11:10; Mark 1:2; Luke 7:27
Mal. 4:5, "Behold, I will send you Elijah..." Matt 11:13-14; Matt 17:10-13;
Mark 9:11-13; Luke 1:16-17

E. JESUS STUDY CHARTS

The following is a list of forty-five Old and New Testament study charts that contain **information about Jesus, His life and His ministry.** The list is in Biblical, chronological order. Beneath each title is a brief description of what the chart contains. Be sure to read the accompanying footnotes connected with each Scripture reference given. The charts can be located by turning to the Index to Charts found after the book of Revelation.

OLD TESTAMENT CHARTS

- **WOMEN IN JESUS' FAMILY TREE**
  A list of four Old Testament women: Tamar, Rahab, Ruth and Bathsheba.
- **PARALLELS BETWEEN JOSEPH AND JESUS**
  Seventeen Old Testament references in the Book of Genesis and their New Testament parallels.
- **JESUS AND THE TEN COMMANDMENTS**
  Commandment references from the Book of Exodus and their parallels found in the Gospels.
- **THE OFFERINGS**
  Five offerings the Israelites made to God, their purpose and significance compared to Christ the perfect offering.
- **OLD/NEW SYSTEM OF SACRIFICE**
  Nine comparisons of Old and New Testament sacrifice.
- **THE SNAKE IN THE DESERT**

Old and New Testament comparison. Looking to the snake verses looking to Christ

- **JOB AND JESUS**
  Old and New Testament comparison. Job's questions and problems are answered perfectly in Jesus Christ.
- **CHRIST IN THE PSALMS**
  Nineteen key references to Jesus and their fulfillment in the New Testament.
- **NAMES FOR MESSIAH**
  The four Names Isaiah used to describe the Messiah.

NEW TESTAMENT CHARTS

- **THE TEMPTATIONS**
  The temptations of Jesus and how He used Scripture to combat them.
- **SIX WAYS TO THINK LIKE CHRIST**
  Based in Matthew 5, Jesus points out what kind of lives would be required of His followers.
- **JESUS AND THE OLD TESTAMENT LAW**
  Old and New Testament comparisons. Examples of Old Testament mercy and justice.
- **THE COST OF FOLLOWING JESUS**
  Jesus helped his disciples prepare for the rejection many of them would experience by being Christians.
  Four categories listed with Scripture references.
- **JESUS AND FORGIVENESS**
  Some examples of His willingness to forgive that can be an encouragement to recognize His willingness to forgive us also.
- **THE SEVEN LAST WORDS OF JESUS ON THE CROSS**
  They capture the last moments of Jesus and some of what He went through to gain our forgiveness.
- **HOW JESUS' TRIAL WAS ILLEGAL**
  Six insights listed. Examples of actions taken by the religious leaders that were illegal according to their own laws.
- **THE TOUCH OF JESUS**
  Demonstrates how Jesus cares equally for all. No person is beyond His loving touch.
- **REAL LEADERSHIP**
  Herod compared to Jesus. Based in the Gospel of Mark.
- **KEY CHARACTERISTICS OF CHRIST IN THE GOSPEL**
  Twelve listed with references.
- **WHAT JESUS SAID ABOUT LOVE**
  Nineteen insights with references.
- **JESUS' PROPHECIES IN THE OLIVET DISCOURSE**
  The last days and the second coming. Old and New Testament references.
- **MAJOR EVENTS OF PASSION WEEK**
  Sixteen entries with references
- **WHY DID JESUS HAVE TO DIE?**
  The problem, why Jesus could help, the solution, the results.
- **EVIDENCE THAT JESUS ACTUALLY DIED AND ROSE**
  The evidence given demonstrates Jesus' uniqueness in history

and proves He is the Son of God. Explanations and references included.

- **JESUS AND WOMEN**
  Twelve listings with references
- **SEVEN SABBATH MIRACLES**
  Seven times Jesus healed on the Sabbath challenging the religious leaders to look beneath their rules to their true purpose to honor God by helping those in need.
  God would not have been pleased if Jesus had ignored these people.
- **JESUS' TRIAL**
  Relates each event, probable reasons for each event and extensive references.
  Also contains a short reflection about the trial.
- **OLD TESTAMENT PASSAGES QUOTED BY JESUS**
  Listed on CD-ROM Version
- **CLAIMS OF CHRIST**
  Nine claims mentioned, each with extensive references in the four gospels.
- **NAMES OF JESUS**
  Eight names found in the book of John along with the significance of each.
- **GREAT EXPECTATIONS**
  Wherever He went, Jesus exceeded people's expectations.
  Relates what was expected and what Jesus did with references.
- **SIX STAGES OF JESUS' TRIAL**
  Although Jesus' trial lasted less than eighteen hours, He was taken to six different hearings.
  References and insights given.
- **JESUS' APPEARANCES AFTER HIS RESURRECTION**
  Eleven listings with references.
- **A HARMONY OF THE GOSPELS**
  Two hundred fifty titles of key events with reference and cross reference.
  A great help to locate key references as well as better visualize the travels of Jesus.
- **JESUS' MIRACLES**
  Jesus' miracles found in the gospels. Reference and cross reference given.
  The supernatural events that pointed people to God. Acts of love by One Who is love.
- **THE PARABLES OF JESUS**
  Ten topics listed along with sub headings and references.
- **MESSIANIC PROPHECIES AND THEIR FULFILLMENT**
  Eighteen listed with Old and New Testament references.
- **OUR TRUE IDENTITY IN CHRIST**
  Twenty-four statements with Scripture references.
- **OUR LIVES BEFORE AND AFTER CHRIST**
  Six statements describing our lives before and after Christ.
- **FROM DEATH TO LIFE**
  Insights into what happens when we choose to let Jesus be Lord of our lives.
  Christ is the key.
- **THE EVENTS OF CHRIST'S RETURN**
  Five are listed, based in 1 Thessalonians.
- **CHRIST AND THE ANGELS**

Based in Hebrews chapter 1 and Psalms.
Demonstrates Christ's greatness in comparison to the angels.

- **LESSONS FROM CHRIST'S HUMANITY**
  Five listed: leader, model, sacrifice, conqueror, and high priest. Found in the book of Hebrews.
- **THE OLD AND NEW COVENANT**
  Four categories, eleven Scripture references show the connection between the old Mosaic covenant and the new Messianic covenant.
- **NAMES OF JESUS**
  Nineteen listed in the book of Revelation. Each one tells something of His character and highlights a particular aspect of His role within God's plan of redemption.

A last word about Jesus. Whenever I think of Him, these stories come to mind.

<u>The Upward Climb Depends on the One Who went ahead.</u>

Two mountain climbers were going to attempt to climb the Matterhorn, this steep mountain in the Alps is over 14,000 feet high. They hired three guides and as they started to climb they attached safety ropes between them. The strongest and most experienced guide went ahead, then a traveler was next, another guide, another traveler and the last guide. As they started to climb the steepest part of the mountain the last man lost his footing and was temporarily held by the other four. The second man started to slip and he pulled down the two above him. The only one left standing was the first guide. He had driven a stake deep into the ground and held his position. He literally held all the others as they dangled in mid-air. His act saved the men and gradually they regained their footing. Can you see the spiritual principle? On the mountain of life we have a strong and experienced Guide, Who has gone before us, Jesus. He has taken a stake in the form of a Cross and plunged it deep into the ground. All who come after Him are held secure by its power. They may slip, they may slide, and they may even fall. But they can never be lost because Jesus, Who went ahead, stands firm through the power of the Cross.

How could you touch others with the extensive knowledge of Jesus in this study guide?

The Attack of the Black Mamba

It happened in Kenya, East Africa. A young girl was walking down a road not far from her home, when she fell into a drainage ditch and broke her leg. An older woman from a nearby village, whom all the children called Mama Geri, climbed down into the ditch to help her. Suddenly they realized they were not alone. With them in the ditch was one of the deadliest predators known in Africa, the Black Mamba. This snake with one strike can inject enough venom to kill twenty men. The snake lifted its head to strike the little girl. Without hesitation Mama Geri stepped in between the snake and the girl. Mama Geri took the full force of the snake's strike. All it's venom was poured out on her. The snake turned and bit the little girl, but now the snake only had it's bite. It had no more venom. It's sting was gone. Although Mama Geri died from the strike, the little girl fully recovered.

There is a great spiritual principle here. The enemy, Satan the serpent, came for you. As he rose up to strike, Jesus stepped in between. Jesus took the full fury of the enemy's strike. All of the enemy's venom was poured out on Jesus upon the Cross. Now the serpent can only bite. He can no longer kill. With Apostle Paul we can now say *(1 Corinthians 15:54-57) "Death is swallowed up in victory. Oh Death, where is your victory? Oh Death, where is your sting?" For sin is the sting that results in death, and the law gives sin its power. How we thank God, Who gives us victory over sin and death through Jesus Christ our Lord!*

STUDY GUIDE #5
AN OVERVIEW OF THE FOUR MAJOR INDEXES AND THE DICTIONARY CONCORDANCE

THE CHRISTIAN WORKER'S RESOURCE is found after the book of Revelation. It contains nineteen pages of supplementary material of varying topics:

- How to Become a Christian
- How to Follow Up with a New Believer
- Mining the Resources of the Life Application Bible
- So You've Been asked to Speak
- Taking the Step to Application

This is followed by a 365 Day Reading Plan

THE FOUR MAJOR INDEXES AND A DICTIONARY CONCORDANCE are found in the back of the Life Application Bible after the book of Revelation.

1. The first and most important index is **THE INDEX TO NOTES OR MASTER INDEX.** This is a list of more than 10,000 notes, referred to as the footnotes, in alphabetical order. It gives the Scripture reference (chapter and verse) as well as the page number for each topic, subject or person listed. It contains over one hundred pages. It also lists <u>charts, maps and personality profiles.</u>

2. The second major index is **THE INDEX TO CHARTS.** It follows the Index to Notes and contains more than two hundred and sixty charts listed in chronological order. That is the order in which they are found in the Bible, starting with the charts in the book of Genesis and ending with the charts found in the book of Revelation.

3. The third major index is **THE INDEX TO MAPS.** This follows the Index to Charts. All the maps are listed in chronological order, starting with the maps in the book of Genesis and ending with those in the book of Revelation. This index contains more than two hundred maps. The name of each map is listed along with the page number on which it is found.

4. The fourth major index is **THE INDEX TO PERSONALITY PROFILES.** It follows the Index to Maps. It could also be called The Index to Bible Characters or Bible People. Each Bible character is listed in alphabetical order, beginning with Aaron and ending with Zerubbabel. Each person's profile is listed along with the page number on which it can be found. The index contains more than one hundred and fifteen personality profiles.

DICTIONARY CONCORDANCE

The dictionary concordance is found after the Index to Personality Profiles. It is not a complete concordance but an abbreviated one. The concordance is set up like a dictionary; has a list of subjects or topics in alphabetical order and gives a short definition of each. It also lists some of the chapter and verse references where it is used.

Take Note: this is different from the Index to Notes that contains all the footnotes.

CHAPTER 3 LEARNING ABOUT PEOPLE OF THE BIBLE

SECTION 1 PERSONALITY PROFILES

One of the most loved features of the Life Application Bible is the Personality Profiles, also referred to as the study of people of the Bible. We note that some of these Bible people are rich in wisdom and understanding; they spur us on to faith, heroism, service of God and good deeds. Many times by their mistakes they instruct us in what not to do. They provide a contrast in making wrong choices and decisions verses the right ones.

There are more than 115 personality profiles in the Life Application Bible. The Index to these profiles is located in the back of the Life Application Bible after the book of Revelation.

Take time to read the personality profile of King David found on the next page. Note there are seven categories of information found in a personality profile. Each category has a circled number beside it from one to seven.

1. General Summary (Untitled category)
2. Strengths and accomplishments
3. Weaknesses and mistakes
4. Lessons from his/her life
5. Vital Statistics
6. Key Verses
7. Where the character's story is told (untitled category)

You will notice two of the categories are untitled, number one *General Summary* and number seven *Where the character's story is told in the Bible*. We have assigned a title to each of these to make it clear and defined for your study.

1 When we think of David, we think: shepherd, poet, giant-killer, king, ancestor of Jesus—in short, one of the greatest men in the Old Testament. But alongside that list stands another: betrayer, liar, adulterer, murderer. The first list gives qualities we all might like to have; the second, qualities that might be true of any one of us. The Bible makes no effort to hide David's failures. Yet he is remembered and respected for his heart for God. Knowing how much more we share in David's failures than in his greatness, we should be curious to find out what made God refer to David as "a man after my own heart" (Acts 13:22).

David, more than anything else, had an unchangeable belief in the faithful and forgiving nature of God. He was a man who lived with great zest. He sinned, but he was quick to confess his sins. His confessions were from the heart, and his repentance was genuine. David never took God's forgiveness lightly or his blessing for granted. In return, God never held back from David either his forgiveness or the consequences of his actions. David experienced the joy of forgiveness even when he had to suffer the consequences of his sins.

We tend to get these two reversed. Too often we would rather avoid the consequences than experience forgiveness. Another big difference between us and David is that while he sinned greatly, he did not sin repeatedly. He learned from his mistakes because he accepted the suffering they brought. Often we don't seem to learn from our mistakes or the consequences that result from those mistakes. What changes would it take for God to find this kind of obedience in you?

2 **Strengths and accomplishments**
- Greatest king of Israel
- Ancestor of Jesus Christ
- Listed in the Hall of Faith in Hebrews 11
- A man described by God himself as a man after his own heart

3 **Weaknesses and mistakes**
- Committed adultery with Bathsheba
- Arranged the murder of Uriah, Bathsheba's husband
- Directly disobeyed God in taking a census of the people
- Did not deal decisively with the sins of his children

4 **Lessons from his life**
- Willingness to honestly admit our mistakes is the first step in dealing with them
- Forgiveness does not remove the consequences of sin
- God greatly desires our complete trust and worship

5 **Vital statistics**
- Where: Bethlehem, Jerusalem
- Occupations: Shepherd, musician, poet, soldier, king
- Relatives: Father: Jesse. Wives: included Michal, Ahinoam, Bathsheba, Abigail. Sons: included Absalom, Amnon, Solomon, Adonijah. Daughters: included Tamar. Seven brothers
- Contemporaries: Saul, Jonathan, Samuel, Nathan

6 **Key verses**
"For you are God, O Sovereign LORD. Your words are truth, and you have promised these good things to me, your servant. And now, may it please you to bless me and my family so that our dynasty may continue forever before you. For when you grant a blessing to your servant, O Sovereign LORD, it is an eternal blessing!" (2 Samuel 7:28, 29).

7 His story is told in 1 Samuel 16—1 Kings 2. He is also mentioned in Amos 6:5; Matthew 1:1, 6; 22:43-45; Luke 1:32; Acts 13:22; Romans 1:3; Hebrews 11:32.

HOW ARE THESE CATEGORIES HELPFUL TO US?

Knowing these categories will help us to

1. Personally understand the life of the character.
2. Recognize similarities in our own life like strengths and weaknesses, etc.
3. Be inspired by their faith during trials and adversity.
4. Gain knowledge we can use to effectively prepare teachings on Bible characters.
5. Teach others how to use the personality profiles.

What other ways are these categories helpful to us?

The profiles can help us construct teaching or Bible study outlines that flow in a logical progression and are easily understandable.

What other ways could you use these profiles?

<u>LARGE GROUP EXERCISE</u>

The following is an exercise that can be used in a large group setting where everyone has a Life Application Bible. We have used this exercise in our seminars all over the world. It is great fun and enjoyed by both teachers and participants alike.

ASK THE QUESTION: Who besides Jesus is your favorite Bible character?

1. As a name is called out ask, "How many others choose that name?"
2. Have them stand, group together and go to one part of the room with their Life Application Bibles.
3. Repeat this process until there are approximately 5 to 10 characters and groups throughout the room.
   Write down the names of the characters so presenter knows about whom the groups are reading.
   Point to each group and have them call out the name of their character.
4. Direct the groups to turn to the Index to Personality Profiles found in the back of the Bible after Index to Maps.
5. Have each group locate the Bible character they have selected and turn to the page where their character's personality profile is found.
6. Instruct them to silently read the information found in the personality profile their character.

<u>THEN STATE:</u> You have **<u>just had a personal experience</u>** of learning about one of your favorite Bible characters. **Choose a representative** from your group and using what you have just read in the personality profile give a short report about your character.

As you point to each group, have them call out the name of their character and then give their report. All who share receive a small prize, a pen, pencil or a small candy bar, along with a round of applause.

Have everyone return to their seat to **<u>record in their notes some of the information and insights they have just learned</u>**.

PERSONALITY PROFILES ALTERNATE EXERCISE

1. Turn to the Index to Personality Profiles found after the book of Revelation.
2. Select the character you find most interesting or your favorite character
3. Take time and read that character's personality profile.
4. For your report write down any of the following
    - Any new and interesting discoveries about this person
    - Similarities between the character's life and your life
    - Lessons from his or her life you can apply personally
    - Weaknesses you would like to improve upon
    - Strengths you would like to develop

Sometimes when we read the personality profiles we discover similarities between the characters and ourselves. We become aware of things in our lives that we would like to change. This provides an opportunity to eliminate negative characteristics and develop positive ones.

Studying people of the Bible having great fun on the island of Curacao

During this large group exercise some of the participants chose the Old Testament character of Joseph for their research. They all read the personality profile in the Life Application Bible with its extensive information. They decided for their presentation they would have one spokesperson at the microphone relate the events in the life of Joseph and a team of ten others act out those events. They all did an excellent job portraying Joseph's coat of many colors, his being put down a well and his being sold into slavery by his brothers. When they acted out the scene of Potiphar's wife chasing Joseph around the stage trying to seduce him, it brought the house down with laughter and applause. They showed us how much fun studying people of the Bible could be.

CHAPTER 3 LEARNING ABOUT PEOPLE OF THE BIBLE

The following is a teaching outline prepared for you on the life of David using some of the categories in the personality profile. This example can be used as a pattern to create teaching outlines using other Bible characters of interest to you.

COMPLETED EXAMPLE:

Being convinced of the great benefits gained from studying the lives of bible characters, Pat agreed to present a teaching using the personality profile of David. She

1. located David in the Index to Personality Profiles
2. read the profile taking note of the sections on his strengths and accomplishments, weaknesses and mistakes, and the lessons from his life.

Using that information Pat prepared the following teaching outline.

David had many strengths and accomplishments

1. he was the greatest king of Israel
2. he was an ancestor of Jesus
3. he is listed in the hall of faith in Hebrews 11
4. he is described by God Himself as a man after God's own heart

He made many mistakes and he greatly sinned and offended God by

1. committing adultery with Bathsheba
2. arranging the murder of Uriah, her husband
3. directly disobeying God by taking a census of the people
4. not dealing directly with the sins of his children

Lessons learned from David's life are

1. a willingness to honestly admit our mistakes is the first step in dealing with them
2. forgiveness does not remove the consequences of sin
3. God greatly desires our complete trust and worship

Understanding the life of David can help us

1. be inspired by his faithfulness,in the midst of tremendous adversity, he always trusted God and sought His presence

2. imitate his sincere repentance, in spite of serious sins God will never fail to forgive and cleanse
3. pray for a love of God as deep as David's
   it takes a tremendous love of God to be called a man after God's own heart.

<u>TESTIMONY OF A CUBAN PASTOR</u>

During a Life Application Bible Seminar in Cuba, one pastor rejoiced, "It took me hours of study to research a single character or person of the Bible. I had to go through several books. Now with the personality profile I have a summary of the information I need on one page. This will be a great help for me in my personal study and also in my teaching at church.

***HOME STUDY CHALLENGE

PREPARING A TEACHING OUTLINE ON A BIBLE CHARACTER

Turn to the Index to Personality Profiles found at the end of the Bible after the book of Revelation. It is the last index before the section containing maps and the concordance.

a. Select a bible character.
b. Turn to the page where his or her profile is found.
c. Read the complete profile, taking note of the sections on strengths and weaknesses, and the lessons from the characters life.
d. Prepare a teaching outline similar to the previous example of David. Include some of the strengths and accomplishments, weaknesses and mistakes as well as the lessons learned from this character's life.
e. Add your reflections and comments as well.

STUDY GUIDE # 6 CHARTS ABOUT BIBLE PEOPLE

The focus of this study is to provide a list of key charts about Bible people. Any of the charts on this page can be developed into a lesson for Bible study. Be sure to read all footnotes and cross references to enrich your presentation. All of the following titles can be found in the Index to Charts.

A. **WHO'S WHO IN THE BIBLE**
This chart provides a list of some of the people found in the genealogies of 1 Chronicles chapters 1-5. It contains 27 characters along with a key lesson from their life and where in the Scripture their full story is told.

B. **THE TWELVE DISCIPLES**
This informative chart is found in Mark 3. It is also found in the Index to Notes under the heading "Disciples". It gives the disciple's name, occupation, outstanding traits, major events in his life, what Jesus said about him, a key lesson from his life as well as a chapter and verse reference. This section is especially useful in presenting an overview of the life of the twelve disciples and their interaction with Jesus.

C. **GREAT ESCAPES IN THE BIBLE**
Located in Acts 9 This chart is also listed in the Index to Notes under "Escape". This interesting chart would enliven any Bible study and captivate the curious. It highlights the great escapes of 10 Bible characters and how God's plans were fulfilled. It provides chapter and verse reference, what actually happened, what the escape accomplished and its application for us today.

D. **BIBLE PERSECUTIONS**
Located around 2 Chronicles 18 and listed in the Index to Notes under "Persecutions". This two-page chart deals with persecutions of Old and New Testament characters, who persecuted them, why they were persecuted, the result of the persecution and the scriptural reference. The chart shows that persecution comes from a variety of people and is given in a variety of ways.

E. **GOD USES COMMON PEOPLE**

Located in Judges 6. In the Index to Notes this chart is listed under the word "Ordinary" and titled "God Uses Ordinary People". It is also listed in the Index to Charts and titled "God Uses Common People". This chart contains a list of thirteen ordinary people who were used by God in extraordinary ways, the task they performed and a scripture reference. Reading the chart gives affirmation and encouragement to ordinary people who would dare to believe that God could use them to accomplish great things in His service.

F. **WHO WERE THESE PROPHETS**

Located in 2 Kings 17 and listed in the Index to Charts under the title "The Prophets of Israel & Judah". This extensive chart spans two pages and provides a brief description of 18 key Old Testament prophets. The information includes the prophet's name, time of ministry, under whose reign they ministered, their main message and its significance.

G. **KEY CHARACTERISTICS OF CHRIST IN THE GOSPELS**

Found in Mark 11 and also in the Index to Notes under the heading "Jesus Christ". This excellent chart contains 12 characteristics of Jesus that reveal insights about His life and ministry. Using the Scripture reference provided, each characteristic can become an interesting subject for a bible study.

CHAPTER 3 LEARNING ABOUT PEOPLE OF THE BIBLE

SECTION 2 HOME STUDY CHALLENGE

KEY CHARACTERISTICS OF CHRIST IN THE GOSPELS

The focus of this study is to help you become familiar with the chart called Key Characteristics of Christ in the Gospels.

1. Turn to the chart located in Mark 11
2. Select one of the twelve key characteristics of Jesus
3. Read the passage and any related footnotes containing references to the characteristic you are studying
   NOTE: a footnote could begin a verse or two before the verse given and continue a verse or two after. So be sure to consider those footnotes as well
4. Write down what wisdom, insight or new understanding you have gained from your research. Record your personal reflections

COMPLETED EXAMPLE: Michelle selected **Jesus was Compassionate** for her research.

She used the Scripture reference Mark 1:40-42 A man with leprosy came to him and begged him on his knees, "If you are willing, you can make me clean." **Filled with compassion, Jesus reached out His hand and touched the man. "I am willing," he said, "Be clean!"** Immediately the leprosy left him and he was cured.

Michelle shared from the footnote that Jesus, in His compassion, touched this man even though lepers were considered unclean and unfit to participate in any religious or social activity. The footnote states, "The real value of a person is inside; not outside. Although a person's body may be diseased or deformed, the person inside is no less valuable to God. No person is too disgusting for God's touch. When you feel repulsed by someone, stop and remember how God feels about that person and about you."

Wherever we go we experience a tremendous hunger for God's Word. A Life Application Bible Seminar in the Yucatan Peninsula Region of Mexico with the Mayan Indians was no exception. Following are some of the pictures of that seminar and the story of one hungry boy.

The seminar was well attended in the small village of Xcan. As in every seminar we had a rule that participants had to be at least seventeen years old to receive a Life Application Bible. A fifteen-year-old boy asked if he could please come in and just sit with his friends and listen as we taught. He sat in the front row and was totally absorbed and attentive. He tried to answer our questions and participate in every way. His hunger to learn was moving. Having only a ballpoint pen he began taking notes by writing them on his arm. We were touched by his hunger so we overlooked the age requirement and gifted him with his own Life Application Bible and notebook. At the end of the seminar he was recognized before the whole class as one of the most attentive and dedicated students.

CHAPTER 4 LOCATING, DEFINING AND USING THE FEATURES OF THE LIFE APPLICATION BIBLE

SECTION 1 A TREASURE HUNT

The focus of this study is to familiarize you with the features found within the Life Application Bible.

REMEMBER: A FEATURE is a study tool, a reference tool, or a teaching tool.

THINK OF IT AS A TREASURE HUNT

Psalm 119:111 says: Your words are a treasure. They are truly my heart's delight.

Psalm 119:162 says: I rejoice in Your Word like one who finds a great treasure.

You are going on a treasure hunt in the Life Application Bible. You are going to search for keys that unlock the treasure of God's Word. The keys you are searching for are the different features and study helps that illuminate God's Word.

Take time to look at the eleven features in **Study Guide #7** that begins on the next page and read the definition of each feature. Once you have read the names of the features and their definitions begin to locate them in the Matthew portion of Scripture that follows the study guide. When you locate a feature in the Matthew portion write the number of the feature next to its name. For example: feature number one is Blueprint, an overall plan of the book in outline form. Write the number one next to Blueprint in the Matthew portion. Now go on to feature number two which is a Chart. Read the definition of a chart, locate a chart in the Matthew portion, and write the number two next to the chart. That indicates you have successfully found the second feature. Continue on until you have found all eleven features in the Matthew portion and have written the corresponding number next to the feature.

STUDY GUIDE #7	DEFINITION OF FEATURES

1. **BLUEPRINT** - Overall plan of the book in outline form

2. **CHART** - A list in outline form that may describe one of the following:
    a. the Person, Power or Plan of God
    b. the action of Bible characters
    c. historical information
    d. a spiritual truth
    e. how to put God's Word into action today

The Index to Charts is located in the back of the Bible

3. **CROSS REFERENCE** - Found in the margins, gives a similar passage located in another place in the Bible

4. **MAPS** - A built in Bible atlas. There are three kinds of maps
    a. **key places** - located at the beginning of a book gives a picture story of key places in that book
    b. **thumbnail maps** - located in the footnotes showing geographical movements in the Bible
    c. **general maps** - located in the back of the Bible detail locations of key importance, events, OT empires, Jesus' ministry, Apostles travels, Paul's journeys, the world today

The Index to Maps is located in the back of the Bible

5. **MEGATHEMES** - means big themes or great themes
    a. gives the main theme of a book of the bible
    b. tells why it is still important today

6. **NOTES OR FOOTNOTES** - found at the bottom of the page footnotes tell more about a verse in one of two ways

   a. **explanatory note** - helps understand more about culture, history, background, places, theological concepts, etc.

   b. **application note** - gives some ideas for putting God's Word into action in our lives today

The Index to Notes is located in the back of the Bible

7. **OVERVIEW** - located in the book introduction section This is a quick look at a book of the Bible, a brief summary.

8. **PERSONALITY PROFILES** - a short or condensed study of some people in the Bible a character study in brief

The Index to Personality Profiles is located in the back of the Bible

9. **TEXTUAL NOTES** - found at the bottom of the page in extra fine print with bold, lower case letters in alphabetical order. Textual notes provide explanations of certain wording in the translation, as well as alternate translations and information from ancient manuscripts.

10. **TIMELINE** - a timeline is a chronological list that puts people and events in order of their appearance in that particular book

    a. located across the top of the page at the beginning of some books

    b. located in the front of the bible a chronological list arranged to show the events of the bible in relationship to world history

11. **VITAL STATISTICS** - located at the beginning of each book presents key facts about the book like

    a. the purpose
    b. the author
    c. the date written
    d. the setting

MATTHEW

Herod the Great begins to rule 37 B.C.	Jesus is born 6/5 B.C.	Escape to Egypt 5/4 B.C.	Herod the Great dies 4 B.C.	Return to Nazareth 4/3 B.C.	Judea becomes a Roman province A.D. 6	Jesus visits Temple as a boy 6/7

VITAL STATISTICS

PURPOSE:
To prove that Jesus is the Messiah, the eternal King

AUTHOR:
Matthew (Levi)

TO WHOM WRITTEN:
Matthew wrote especially to the Jews

DATE WRITTEN:
Approximately A.D. 60–65

SETTING:
Matthew was a Jewish tax collector who became one of Jesus' disciples. This Gospel forms the connecting link between the Old and New Testaments because of its emphasis on the fulfillment of prophecy.

KEY VERSE:
"Don't misunderstand why I have come. I did not come to abolish the law of Moses or the writings of the prophets. No, I came to fulfill them" (5:17).

KEY PEOPLE:
Jesus, Mary, Joseph, John the Baptist, the disciples, the religious leaders, Caiaphas, Pilate, Mary Magdalene

KEY PLACES:
Bethlehem, Jerusalem, Capernaum, Galilee, Judea

SPECIAL FEATURES:
Matthew is filled with messianic language ("Son of David" is used throughout) and Old Testament references (53 quotes and 76 other references). This Gospel was not written as a chronological account; its purpose was to present the clear evidence that Jesus is the Messiah, the Savior.

Overview

AS the motorcade slowly winds through the city, thousands pack the sidewalks hoping to catch a glimpse. Marching bands with great fanfare announce the arrival, and protective agents scan the crowd and run alongside the limousine. Pomp, ceremony, protocol—modern symbols of position and evidences of importance—herald the arrival of a head of state. Whether they are leaders by birth or election, we honor and respect them.

The Jews waited for a leader who had been promised centuries before by prophets. They believed that this leader—the Messiah ("anointed one")—would rescue them from their Roman oppressors and establish a new kingdom. As their king, he would rule the world with justice. However, many Jews overlooked prophecies that also spoke of this king as a suffering servant who would be rejected and killed. It is no wonder, then, that few recognized Jesus as the Messiah. How could this humble carpenter's son from Nazareth be their king? But Jesus was and is the King of all the earth!

Matthew (Levi) was one of Jesus' 12 disciples. Once he was a despised tax collector, but his life was changed by this man from Galilee. Matthew wrote this Gospel to his fellow Jews to prove that Jesus is the Messiah and to explain God's Kingdom.

Matthew begins his account by giving Jesus' genealogy. He then tells of Jesus' birth and early years, including the family's escape to Egypt from the murderous Herod and their return to Nazareth. Following Jesus' baptism by John (3:16, 17) and his defeat of Satan in the wilderness, Jesus begins his public ministry by calling his first disciples and giving the Sermon on the Mount (chapters 5—7). Matthew shows Christ's authority by reporting his miracles of healing the sick and the demon-possessed, and even raising the dead.

Despite opposition from the Pharisees and others in the religious establishment (chapters 12—15), Jesus continued to teach concerning the Kingdom of Heaven (chapters 16—20). During this time, Jesus spoke with his disciples about his imminent death and resurrection (16:21) and revealed his true identity to Peter, James, and John (17:1–5). Near the end of his ministry, Jesus entered Jerusalem in a triumphant procession (21:1–11). But soon opposition mounted, and Jesus knew that his death was near. So he taught his disciples about the future—what they could expect before his return (chapter 24) and how to live until then (chapter 25).

In Matthew's finale (chapters 26—28), he focuses on Jesus' final days on earth—the Last Supper, his prayer in Gethsemane, the betrayal by Judas, the flight of the disciples, Peter's denial, the trials before Caiaphas and Pilate, Jesus' final words on the cross, and his burial in a borrowed tomb. But the story does not end there, for the Messiah rose from the dead—conquering death and then telling his followers to continue his work by making disciples in all nations.

As you read this Gospel, listen to Matthew's clear message: Jesus is the Christ, the King of kings and Lord of lords. Celebrate his victory over evil and death, and make Jesus the Lord of your life.

Tiberius Caesar becomes emperor 14	*Pontius Pilate appointed governor 26*	*Jesus begins his ministry 26/27*	*Jesus chooses twelve disciples 28*	*Jesus feeds 5,000 29*	*Jesus is crucified, rises again, and ascends 30*

THE BLUEPRINT

A. BIRTH AND PREPARATION OF JESUS, THE KING (1:1—4:11)

The people of Israel were waiting for the Messiah, their king. Matthew begins his book by showing how Jesus Christ was a descendant of David. But Matthew goes on to show that God did not send Jesus to be an earthly king but a heavenly King. His Kingdom would be much greater than David's because it would never end. Even at Jesus' birth, many recognized him as a King. Herod, the ruler, as well as Satan, was afraid of Jesus' kingship and tried to stop him, but others worshiped him and brought royal gifts. We must be willing to recognize Jesus for who he really is and worship him as King of our life.

B. MESSAGE AND MINISTRY OF JESUS, THE KING (4:12—25:46)

1. Jesus begins his ministry
2. Jesus gives the Sermon on the Mount
3. Jesus performs many miracles
4. Jesus teaches about the Kingdom
5. Jesus encounters differing reactions to his ministry
6. Jesus faces conflict with the religious leaders
7. Jesus teaches on the Mount of Olives

Jesus gave the Sermon on the Mount, directions for living in his Kingdom. He also told many parables about the difference between his Kingdom and the kingdoms of earth. Forgiveness, peace, and putting others first are some of the characteristics that make one great in the Kingdom of God. And to be great in God's Kingdom, we must live by God's standards right now. Jesus came to show us how to live as faithful subjects in his Kingdom.

C. DEATH AND RESURRECTION OF JESUS, THE KING (26:1—28:20)

Jesus was formally presented to the nation of Israel but was rejected. How strange for the King to be accused, arrested, and crucified. But Jesus demonstrated his power, even over death, through his resurrection and gained access for us into his Kingdom. With all this evidence that Jesus is God's Son, we, too, should accept him as our Lord.

MEGATHEMES

THEME	EXPLANATION	IMPORTANCE
Jesus Christ, the King	Jesus is revealed as the King of kings. His miraculous birth, his life and teaching, his miracles, and his triumph over death show his true identity.	Jesus cannot be equated with any person or power. He is the supreme ruler of time and eternity, heaven and earth, humans and angels. We should give him his rightful place as King of our life.
The Messiah	Jesus was the Messiah, the one for whom the Jews had waited to deliver them from Roman oppression. Yet, tragically, they didn't recognize him when he came because his kingship was not what they expected. The true purpose of God's anointed deliverer was to die for all people to free them from sin's oppression.	Because Jesus was sent by God, we can trust him with our life. It is worth everything we have to acknowledge him and give ourselves to him, because he came to be our Messiah, our Savior.
Kingdom of God	Jesus came to earth to begin his Kingdom. His full Kingdom will be realized at his return and will be made up of anyone who has faithfully followed him.	The way to enter God's Kingdom is by faith—believing in Christ to save us from sin and change our life. We must do the work of his Kingdom now to be prepared for his return.

Teachings	Jesus taught the people through sermons, illustrations, and parables. Through his teachings, he showed the true ingredients of faith and how to guard against a fruitless and hypocritical life.	Jesus' teachings show us how to prepare for life in his eternal Kingdom by living properly right now. He lived what he taught, and we, too, must practice what we preach.
Resurrection	When Jesus rose from the dead, he rose in power as the true King. In his victory over death, he established his credentials as King and his power and authority over evil.	The Resurrection shows Jesus' all-powerful life for us—not even death could stop his plan of offering eternal life. Those who believe in Jesus can hope for a resurrection like his. Our role is to tell his story to all the earth so that everyone may share in his victory.

KEY PLACES IN MATTHEW

Maps

Jesus' earthly story begins in the town of Bethlehem in the Roman province of Judea (2:1). A threat to kill the infant king led Joseph to take his family to Egypt (2:14). When they returned, God led them to settle in Nazareth in Galilee (2:22, 23). At about age 30, Jesus was baptized in the Jordan River and was tempted by Satan in the Judean wilderness (3:13; 4:1). Jesus set up his base of operations in Capernaum (4:12, 13) and from there ministered throughout Israel, telling parables, teaching about the Kingdom, and healing the sick. He traveled to Gadara and healed two demon-possessed men (8:28ff); fed over 5,000 people with five loaves and two fish on the shores of Galilee near Bethsaida (14:15ff); healed the sick in Gennesaret (14:34ff); ministered to the Gentiles in Tyre and Sidon (15:21ff); visited Caesarea Philippi, where Peter declared him to be the Messiah (16:13ff); and taught in Perea, across the Jordan (19:1). As he set out on his last visit to Jerusalem, he told the disciples what would happen to him there (20:17ff). He spent some time in Jericho (20:29) and then stayed in Bethany at night as he went back and forth to Jerusalem during his last week (21:17ff). In Jerusalem he would be crucified, but he would rise again.

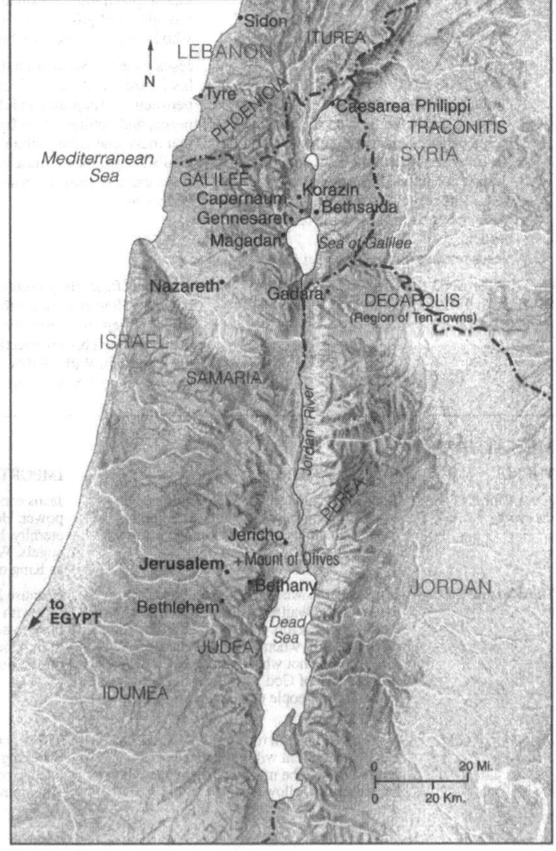

The broken lines (—·—·) indicate modern boundaries.

A. BIRTH AND PREPARATION OF JESUS, THE KING (1:1—4:11)

Matthew opens his Gospel with a genealogy to prove that Jesus is a descendant of both King David and Abraham, just as the Old Testament had predicted. Jesus' birth didn't go unnoticed, for both shepherds and astrologers came to worship him. The Jewish people were waiting for the Messiah to appear. However, after he was born, the Jews didn't recognize him because they were looking for a different kind of king.

The Record of Jesus' Ancestors (**3**/Luke 3:23-38)

1 This is a record of the ancestors of Jesus the Messiah, a descendant of King David and of Abraham:

2 Abraham was the father of Isaac.
Isaac was the father of Jacob.
Jacob was the father of Judah and his brothers.
3 Judah was the father of Perez and Zerah (their mother was Tamar).
Perez was the father of Hezron.
Hezron was the father of Ram.*
4 Ram was the father of Amminadab.
Amminadab was the father of Nahshon.
Nahshon was the father of Salmon.
5 Salmon was the father of Boaz (his mother was Rahab).
Boaz was the father of Obed (his mother was Ruth).
Obed was the father of Jesse.
6 Jesse was the father of King David.
David was the father of Solomon (his mother was Bathsheba, the widow of Uriah).
7 Solomon was the father of Rehoboam.
Rehoboam was the father of Abijah.
Abijah was the father of Asaph.*
8 Asaph was the father of Jehoshaphat.
Jehoshaphat was the father of Jehoram.*
Jehoram was the father* of Uzziah.
9 Uzziah was the father of Jotham.
Jotham was the father of Ahaz.
Ahaz was the father of Hezekiah.
10 Hezekiah was the father of Manasseh.
Manasseh was the father of Amos.*
Amos was the father of Josiah.
11 Josiah was the father of Jehoiachin* and his brothers (born at the time of the exile to Babylon).

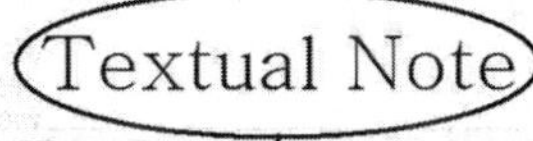

1:1 Gen 22:18; 2 Sam 7:12-14; 1 Chr 17:11; Pss 89:3-4; 132:11; Isa 9:6; 11:1; Matt 22:42; John 7:42; Rom 1:3; Gal 3:16; Rev 22:16
1:2 Gen 21:3, 12; 25:26; 29:35; 1 Chr 1:34
1:3 Gen 38:29-30; Ruth 4:12, 18-19; 1 Chr 2:4-5, 9
1:4-5 Ruth 4:13, 17-22; 1 Chr 2:10-12, 15; Heb 11:31
1:6 Ruth 4:17, 22; 2 Sam 12:24; 1 Chr 2:13-15
1:7-10 1 Chr 3:10-14
1:11 2 Kgs 24:14-16; 1 Chr 3:15-16; Jer 27:20; Dan 1:1-2

1:3 Greek *Aram;* also in 1:4. See 1 Chr 2:9-10. **1:7** *Asaph* is the same person as Asa; also in 1:8. See 1 Chr 3:10. **1:8a** Greek *Joram.* See 1 Kgs 22:50 and note at 1 Chr 3:11. **1:8b** Or *ancestor;* also in 1:11. **1:10** *Amos* is the same person as Amon. See 1 Chr 3:14. **1:11** Greek *Jeconiah;* also in 1:12. See 2 Kgs 24:6 and note at 1 Chr 3:16.

1:1 Presenting this genealogy was one of the most interesting ways that Matthew could begin a book for a Jewish audience. Because a person's family line proved his or her standing as one of God's chosen people, Matthew began by showing that Jesus was a descendant of Abraham, the father of all Jews, and a direct descendant of David, fulfilling Old Testament prophecies about the Messiah's line. The facts of this ancestry were carefully preserved. This is the first of many proofs recorded by Matthew to show that Jesus is the true Messiah.

1:1ff More than 400 years had passed since the last Old Testament prophecies, and faithful Jews all over the world were still waiting for the Messiah (Luke 3:15). Matthew wrote this book to Jews to present Jesus as King and Messiah, the promised descendant of David who would reign forever (Isaiah 11:1-5). The Gospel of Matthew links the Old and New Testaments and contains many references that show how Jesus fulfilled Old Testament prophecy.

1:1ff Jesus entered human history when the land of Palestine was controlled by Rome and considered an insignificant outpost of the vast and mighty Roman Empire. The presence of Roman soldiers in Israel gave the Jews military peace, but at the price of oppression, slavery, injustice, and immorality. Into this kind of world came the promised Messiah.

1:1-17 In the first 17 verses we meet 46 people whose lifetimes span 2,000 years. All were ancestors of Jesus, but they varied considerably in personality, spirituality, and experience. Some were heroes of faith—like Abraham, Isaac, Ruth, and David. Some had shady reputations—like Rahab and Tamar. Many were very ordinary—like Hezron, Ram, Nahshon, and Akim. And others were evil—like Manasseh and Abijah. God's work in history is not limited by human failures or sins, and he works through ordinary people. Just as God used all kinds of people to bring his Son into the world, he uses all kinds today to accomplish his will. And God wants to use you.

1:11 The Exile occurred in 586 B.C. when Nebuchadnezzar, king of Babylon, conquered Judah, destroyed Jerusalem, and took thousands of captives to Babylon.

12 After the Babylonian exile:
Jehoiachin was the father of Shealtiel.
Shealtiel was the father of Zerubbabel.
13 Zerubbabel was the father of Abiud.
Abiud was the father of Eliakim.
Eliakim was the father of Azor.
14 Azor was the father of Zadok.
Zadok was the father of Akim.
Akim was the father of Eliud.
15 Eliud was the father of Eleazar.
Eleazar was the father of Matthan.
Matthan was the father of Jacob.
16 Jacob was the father of Joseph, the husband of Mary.
Mary was the mother of Jesus, who is called the Messiah.

17 All those listed above include fourteen generations from Abraham to King David, and fourteen from David's time to the Babylonian exile, and fourteen from the Babylonian exile to the Messiah.

An Angel Appears to Joseph **(8)**

18 Now this is how Jesus the Messiah was born. His mother, Mary, was engaged to be
married to Joseph. But while she was still a virgin, she became pregnant by the Holy
Spirit. 19 Joseph, her fiancé, being a just man, decided to break the engagement quietly,
so as not to disgrace her publicly.
20 As he considered this, he fell asleep, and an angel of the Lord appeared to him in a
dream. "Joseph, son of David," the angel said, "do not be afraid to go ahead with your
marriage to Mary. For the child within her has been conceived by the Holy Spirit. 21 And

1:12
1 Chr 3:17, 19
Ezra 3:2

Cross Reference

1:16
Matt 27:17, 22
Luke 2:11

1:18
Luke 1:27, 35
Gal 4:4

1:19
Deut 24:1

1:20
Luke 1:35

1:16 Because Mary was a virgin when she became pregnant, Matthew lists Joseph only as the husband of Mary, not the father of Jesus. Matthew's genealogy gives Jesus' legal (or royal) lineage through Joseph. Mary's ancestral line is recorded in Luke 3:23-38. Both Mary and Joseph were direct descendants of David.

Matthew traced the genealogy back to Abraham, while Luke traced it back to Adam. Matthew wrote to the Jews, so Jesus was shown as a descendant of their father, Abraham. Luke wrote to the Gentiles, so he emphasized Jesus as the Savior of all people.

1:17 Matthew breaks Israel's history into three sets of 14 generations, but there were probably more generations than those listed here. Genealogies often compressed history, meaning that not every generation of ancestors was specifically listed. Thus, the phrase *the father of* can also be translated "the ancestor of."

1:18 There were three steps in a Jewish marriage. First, the two families agreed to the union. Second, a public announcement was made. At this point, the couple was "engaged." This was similar to engagement today except that their relationship could be broken only through death or divorce (even though sexual relations were not yet permitted). Third, the couple was married and began living together. Because Mary and Joseph were engaged, Mary's apparent unfaithfulness carried a severe social stigma. According to Jewish civil law, Joseph had a right to divorce her, and the Jewish authorities could have had her stoned to death (Deuteronomy 22:23, 24).

1:18 Why is the Virgin Birth important to the Christian faith? Jesus Christ, God's Son, had to be free from the sinful nature passed on to all other human beings by Adam. Because Jesus was born of a woman, he was a human being; but as the Son of God, Jesus was born without any trace of human sin. Jesus is both fully human and fully divine.

Because Jesus lived as a man, we know that he fully understands our experiences and struggles (Hebrews 4:15, 16). Because he is God, he has the power and authority to deliver us from sin (Colossians 2:13-15). We can tell Jesus all our thoughts, feelings, and needs. He has been where we are now, and he has the ability to help.

1:18-25 Joseph was faced with a difficult choice after discovering that Mary was pregnant. Although he knew that taking Mary as his wife could be humiliating, Joseph chose to obey the angel's command to marry her. His action revealed four admirable qualities: (1) righteousness (1:19), (2) discretion and sensitivity (1:19), (3) responsiveness to God (1:24), and (4) self-discipline (1:25).

1:19 Perhaps Joseph thought he had only two options: divorce Mary quietly or have her stoned. But God gave a third option—marry her (1:20-23). In view of the circumstances, this had not occurred to Joseph. But God often shows us that there are more options available than we think. Although Joseph seemed to be doing the right thing by breaking the engagement, only God's guidance helped him make the best decision. When our decisions affect the lives of others, we must always seek God's wisdom.

1:20 The conception and birth of Jesus Christ are supernatural events beyond human logic or reasoning. Because of this, God sent angels to help certain people understand the significance of what was happening (see 2:13, 19; Luke 1:11, 26; 2:9).

Angels are spiritual beings created by God who help carry out his work on earth. They bring God's messages to people (Luke 1:26), protect God's people (Daniel 6:22), offer encouragement (Genesis 16:7ff), give guidance (Exodus 14:19), carry out punishment (2 Samuel 24:16), patrol the earth (Zechariah 1:9-14), and fight the forces of evil (2 Kings 6:16-18; Revelation 20:1, 2). There are both good and bad angels (Revelation 12:7), but because bad angels are allied with the Devil, or Satan, they have considerably less power and authority than good angels. Eventually the main role of angels will be to offer continuous praise to God (Revelation 7:11, 12).

1:20-23 The angel declared to Joseph that Mary's child was conceived by the Holy Spirit and would be a son. This reveals an important truth about Jesus—he is both God and human. The infinite, unlimited God took on the limitations of humanity so he could live and die for the salvation of all who would believe in him.

1:21 Luke 1:31; 2:11, 21 Acts 5:31; 13:23 Heb 7:25
1:23 †Isa 7:14; 8:8, 10 John 1:14 1 Tim 3:16

she will have a son, and you are to name him Jesus,* for he will save his people from
their sins." 22All of this happened to fulfill the Lord's message through his prophet:

23 "Look! The virgin will conceive a child!
She will give birth to a son,
and he will be called Immanuel*
(meaning, God is with us)."

1:21 *Jesus* means "The LORD saves." 1:23 Isa 7:14; 8:8, 10.

Personality Profile

JOSEPH

The strength of what we believe is measured by how much we are willing to suffer for those beliefs. Joseph was a man with strong beliefs. He was prepared to do what was right, despite the pain he knew it would cause. But Joseph had another trait: He not only tried to do what was right, he also tried to do it in the right way.

When Mary told Joseph about her pregnancy, Joseph knew the child was not his. His respect for Mary's character and the explanation she gave him, as well as her attitude toward the expected child, must have made it hard to think his bride had done something wrong. Still, someone else was the child's father—and it was mind-boggling to accept that the "someone else" was God.

Joseph decided he had to break the engagement, but he was determined to do it in a way that would not cause public shame to Mary. He intended to act with justice and love.

At this point, God sent a messenger to Joseph to confirm Mary's story and open another way of obedience for Joseph—to take Mary as his wife. Joseph obeyed God, married Mary, and honored her virginity until the baby was born.

We do not know how long Joseph lived his role as Jesus' earthly father—he is last mentioned when Jesus was 12 years old. But Joseph trained his son in the trade of carpentry, made sure he had good spiritual training in Nazareth, and took the whole family on the yearly trip to Jerusalem for the Passover, which Jesus continued to observe during his adult years.

Joseph knew Jesus was someone special from the moment he heard the angel's words. His strong belief in that fact and his willingness to follow God's leading empowered him to be Jesus' chosen earthly father.

Strengths and accomplishments
- A man of integrity
- A descendant of King David
- Jesus' legal and earthly father
- A person sensitive to God's guidance and willing to do God's will no matter what the consequence

Lessons from his life
- God honors integrity
- Social position is of little importance when God chooses to use us
- Being obedient to the guidance we have from God leads to more guidance from him
- Feelings are not accurate measures of the rightness or wrongness of an action

Vital statistics
- Where: Nazareth, Bethlehem
- Occupation: Carpenter
- Relatives: Wife: Mary. Children: Jesus, James, Joses, Judas, Simon, and daughters
- Contemporaries: Herod the Great, John the Baptist, Simeon, Anna

Key verses
"Joseph, her fiancé, being a just man, decided to break the engagement quietly, so as not to disgrace her publicly. As he considered this, he fell asleep, and an angel of the Lord appeared to him in a dream. 'Joseph, son of David,' the angel said, 'do not be afraid to go ahead with your marriage to Mary. For the child within her has been conceived by the Holy Spirit' " (Matthew 1:19, 20).

Joseph's story is told in Matthew 1:16—2:23; Luke 1:26—2:52.

1:21 *Jesus* means "the Lord saves." Jesus came to earth to save us because we can't save ourselves from sin and its consequences. No matter how good we are, we can't eliminate the sinful nature present in all of us. Only Jesus can do that. Jesus didn't come to help people save themselves; he came to be their Savior from the power and penalty of sin. Thank Christ for his death on the cross for your sin, and then ask him to take control of your life. Your new life begins at that moment.

1:23 Jesus was to be called *Immanuel* ("God is with us"), as predicted by Isaiah the prophet (Isaiah 7:14). Jesus was God in the flesh; thus, God was literally among us, "with us." Through the Holy Spirit, Christ is present today in the life of every believer. Perhaps not even Isaiah understood how far-reaching the meaning of *Immanuel* would be.

24 When Joseph woke up, he did what the angel of the Lord commanded. He brought 1:25
Mary home to be his wife, 25 but she remained a virgin until her son was born. And Luke 1:31
Joseph named him Jesus.

Visitors Arrive from Eastern Lands (**12**)

2 Jesus was born in the town of Bethlehem in Judea, during the reign of King Herod. 2:1
About that time some wise men* from eastern lands arrived in Jerusalem, asking, Luke 1:5; 2:4-7
2 "Where is the newborn king of the Jews? We have seen his star as it arose,* and we 2:2
have come to worship him." Num 24:17
Jer 23:5
3 Herod was deeply disturbed by their question, as was all of Jerusalem. 4 He called a Matt 2:9
meeting of the leading priests and teachers of religious law. "Where did the prophets say Rev 22:16
the Messiah would be born?" he asked them.

2:1 Or *royal astrologers;* Greek reads *magi;* also in 2:7, 16. **2:2** Or *in the east.* Footnote

1:24 Joseph changed his plans quickly after learning that Mary had not been unfaithful to him (1:19). He obeyed God and proceeded with the marriage plans. Although others may have disapproved of his decision, Joseph went ahead with what he knew was right. Sometimes we avoid doing what is right because of what others might think. Like Joseph, we must choose to obey God rather than seek the approval of others.

2:1 Bethlehem is a small town five miles south of Jerusalem. It sits on a high ridge over 2,000 feet above sea level. It is mentioned in more detail in the Gospel of Luke. Luke also explains why Joseph and Mary were in Bethlehem when Jesus was born, rather than in Nazareth, their hometown.

2:1 The land of Israel was divided into four political districts and several lesser territories. Judea was to the south, Samaria in the middle, Galilee to the north, and Idumea to the southwest. Bethlehem of Judea (also called Judah, 2:6) had been prophesied as the Messiah's birthplace (Micah 5:2). Jerusalem was also in Judea and was the seat of government for Herod the Great, king over all four political districts. After Herod's death, the districts were divided among three separate rulers (see the note on 2:19-22). Although he was a ruthless, evil man who murdered many in his own family, Herod the Great supervised the renovation of the Temple, making it much larger and more beautiful. This made him popular with many Jews. Jesus would visit Jerusalem many times because the great Jewish festivals were held there.

2:1, 2 Not much is known about these astrologers (traditionally called wise men). We don't know where they came from or how many there were. Tradition says they were men of high position from Parthia, near the site of ancient Babylon. How did they know that the star represented the Messiah? (1) They could have been Jews who remained in Babylon after the Exile and knew the Old Testament predictions of the Messiah's coming. (2) They may have been eastern astrologers who studied ancient manuscripts from around the world. Because of the Jewish exile centuries earlier, they would have had copies of the Old Testament in their land. (3) They may have had a special message from God directing them to the Messiah. Some scholars say these astrologers were each from a different land, representing the entire world bowing before Jesus. These men from faraway lands recognized Jesus as the Messiah when most of God's chosen people in Israel did not. Matthew pictures Jesus as the King over the whole world, not just Judea.

2:1, 2 The astrologers traveled thousands of miles to see the king of the Jews. When they finally found him, they responded with joy, worship, and gifts. This is so different from the approach people often take today. We expect God to come looking for us, to explain himself, prove who he is, and give *us* gifts. But those who are wise still seek and worship Jesus today, not for what they can get, but for who he is.

2:2 The astrologers said they saw Jesus' star. Balaam referred to a coming "star . . . from Jacob" (Numbers 24:17). Some say this star may have been a conjunction of Jupiter, Saturn, and Mars in 6 B.C., and others offer other explanations. But couldn't God, who created the heavens, have created a special star to signal the arrival of his Son? Whatever the nature of the star, these astrologers traveled thousands of miles searching for a king, and they found him.

2:3 Herod the Great was quite disturbed when the astrologers asked about a newborn king of the Jews because (1) Herod was not the rightful heir to the throne of David; therefore, many Jews hated him as a usurper. If Jesus really was an heir, trouble would arise. (2) Herod was ruthless, and because of his many enemies, he was suspicious that someone would try to overthrow him. (3) Herod didn't want the Jews, a religious people, to unite around a religious figure. (4) If these astrologers were of Jewish descent and from Parthia (the most powerful region next to Rome), they would have welcomed a Jewish king who could swing the balance of power away from Rome. The land of Israel, far from Rome, would have been easy prey for a nation trying to gain more control.

2:4 The leading priests and teachers of religious law were aware of Micah 5:2 and other prophecies about the Messiah. The astrologers' news troubled Herod because he knew that the Jewish people expected the Messiah to come soon (Luke 3:15). Most Jews expected the Messiah to be a great military and political deliverer, like Alexander the Great. Herod's counselors would have told Herod this. No wonder this ruthless man took no chances and ordered all the baby boys in Bethlehem killed (2:16)!

THE FLIGHT TO EGYPT
Herod planned to kill the baby Jesus, whom he perceived to be a future threat to his position. Warned of this treachery in a dream, Joseph took his family to Egypt until Herod's death, which occurred a year or two later. They then planned to return to Judea, but God led them instead to Nazareth in Galilee.

2:5 John 7:42
2:6 †Mic 5:2

[5]"In Bethlehem," they said, "for this is what the prophet wrote:

6 'O Bethlehem of Judah,
you are not just a lowly village in Judah,
for a ruler will come from you
who will be the shepherd for my people Israel.'*"

[7]Then Herod sent a private message to the wise men, asking them to come see him.
At this meeting he learned the exact time when they first saw the star. [8]Then he told them,
"Go to Bethlehem and search carefully for the child. And when you find him, come back
and tell me so that I can go and worship him, too!"

2:9 Matt 2:2
2:11 Ps 72:10 Isa 60:6
2:12 Matt 2:22

[9]After this interview the wise men went their way. Once again the star appeared to
them, guiding them to Bethlehem. It went ahead of them and stopped over the place
where the child was. [10]When they saw the star, they were filled with joy! [11]They entered
the house where the child and his mother, Mary, were, and they fell down before him and
worshiped him. Then they opened their treasure chests and gave him gifts of gold,
frankincense, and myrrh. [12]But when it was time to leave, they went home another way,
because God had warned them in a dream not to return to Herod.

The Escape to Egypt **(13)**

2:13 Matt 1:20; 2:19

[13]After the wise men were gone, an angel of the Lord appeared to Joseph in a dream.
"Get up and flee to Egypt with the child and his mother," the angel said. "Stay there until

2:6 Mic 5:2; 2 Sam 5:2.

GOSPEL ACCOUNTS FOUND ONLY IN MATTHEW

Chart

Passage	*Subject*
1:20–24	Joseph's dream*
2:1–12	The visit of the astrologers
2:13–15	Escape to Egypt*
2:16–18	Slaughter of the children*
27:3–10	The death of Judas*
27:19	The dream of Pilate's wife
27:52	The other resurrections
28:11–15	The bribery of the guards
28:19, 20	The baptism emphasis in the great commission*

Matthew records nine special events that are not mentioned in any of the other Gospels. In each case, the most apparent reason for Matthew's choice has to do with his purpose in communicating the gospel to Jewish people. Five cases are fulfillments of Old Testament prophecies (marked with asterisks above). The other four would have been of particular interest to the Jews of Matthew's day.

2:5, 6 Matthew often quoted Old Testament prophets. This prophecy, paraphrasing Micah 5:2, had been delivered seven centuries earlier.

2:6 Most religious leaders believed in a literal fulfillment of all Old Testament prophecy; therefore, they believed the Messiah would be born in Bethlehem. Ironically, when Jesus was born, these same religious leaders became his greatest enemies. When the Messiah for whom they had been waiting finally came, they didn't recognize him.

2:8 Herod did not want to worship Christ—he was lying. This was a trick to get the astrologers to return to him and reveal the whereabouts of the newborn king. Herod's plan was to kill Jesus.

2:11 Jesus was probably one or two years old when the astrologers found him. By this time, Mary and Joseph were married, living in a house, and intending to stay in Bethlehem for a while. For more on Joseph and Mary's stay there, see the note on Luke 2:39.

2:11 The astrologers gave these expensive gifts because they were worthy presents for a future king. Bible students have seen in the gifts symbols of Christ's identity and what he would accomplish. Gold was a gift for a king; frankincense was a gift for deity; and myrrh was a spice used to anoint a body for burial. These gifts may have provided the financial resources for the trip to Egypt and back.

2:11 The astrologers brought gifts and worshiped Jesus for who he was. This is the essence of true worship—honoring Christ for who he is and being willing to give him what is valuable to you. Worship God because he is the perfect, just, and almighty Creator of the universe, worthy of the best you have to give.

2:12 After finding Jesus and worshiping him, the astrologers were warned by God not to return through Jerusalem as they had intended. Finding Jesus may mean that your life must take a different direction, one that is responsive and obedient to God's Word. Are you willing to be led a different way?

2:13 This was the second dream or vision that Joseph received from God. Joseph's first dream revealed that Mary's child would be the Messiah (1:20, 21). His second dream told him how to protect the child's life. Although Joseph was not Jesus' natural father, he was Jesus' legal father and was responsible for his safety and well-being. Divine guidance comes only to prepared hearts. Joseph remained receptive to God's guidance.

CHAPTER 4 REVIEW QUESTIONS

2 Timothy 2:15 Study to show thyself approved unto God, a workman that needeth not to be ashamed, rightly dividing the word of truth.

Having studied the features of the Life Application Bible try to answer the following questions from memory. If you can't remember all the answers turn back to the study guide.

1. How many features are in the Life Application Bible?

   ____

2. Try to write down five, seven or all eleven features from memory.

   ____
   ____
   ____
   ____

3. What feature found in the margins gives a similar passage in another place in the Bible?

   ____

4. What are the three types of maps featured in this bible?

   ____

5. What is the overall plan of the book of the bible in outline form called?

   ____
   ____

6. This feature is located in the book introduction section and gives us a quick look at a whole book of the bible. What is it called? ______________________

7. What feature presents a study of some key people in the bible?

____

8. What feature is a chronological list that puts people and events in their historical setting?___________________________________

9. What feature includes key facts about a book of the bible such as purpose, author, date written and setting?

____

TAKE NOTE: When studying the features of the Life Application Bible in a seminar format ask the review questions and have participants answer them from memory.

CHAPTER 4 LARGE GROUP EXERCISE UNDERSTANDING A TIMELINE

Write the following ten names on separate sheets of paper in large letters.
This is the correct order that they are found in the Bible

NOAH, JOSHUA, RUTH, NEHEMIAH, ESTHER, HABAKKUK, HAGGAI, PAUL, TIMOTHY, EUTYCHUS

EXERCISE

1. Ask for ten volunteers to come to the front of the room and hold one of the names.
   Mix up the names and give one to each volunteer.
2. Then ask the group of ten to arrange themselves in the order of their appearance in the Bible. The earliest character found in the Bible would be first; the second would be next and so on until all ten are arranged in the correct order.
3. Once they are satisfied with the arrangement have the volunteers face the class. Ask the class if the volunteers have arranged the names properly. If they have not, ask the class to rearrange the volunteers in the correct order. If the participants are unable to do this, the leader can help them
4. Next ask participants to space the characters across the front of the room using the distance from one side to the other as the full length of time.
   This puts the first character all the way to the left (earliest time) and the last character all the way to the right (more recent time). Explain that the spaces between the characters represent numbers of years between them.
5. Finally, have the participants turn to the timeline in the book of Matthew in the Life Application Bible Explain the parallel.
6. Thank the volunteers who participated in the exercise. Collect the signs, give a small prize (candy, pen or pencil) and have them return to their seats. Everyone receives a round of applause for their participation.

"These are some of the brothers and sisters from different countries who went on the treasure hunt and discovered the treasures in the Life Application Bible."

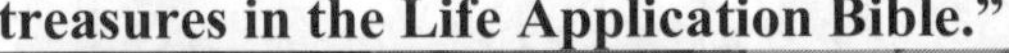

CHAPTER 4

SECTION 2 PREPARING A TEACHING OUTLINE ON A PARTICULAR BOOK OF THE BIBLE

The focus of this study is to help you learn to use the special features known as timelines, vital statistics, overview or general introduction, blueprints and megathemes to prepare a teaching outline on a particular book of the Bible.

EXAMPLE: John chose the book of Isaiah for his study.

a. He noted from the **TIMELINE** that Isaiah became a prophet in 740 B.C. and his ministry ended in 681 B.C.

b. While reviewing the **VITAL STATISTICS** John learned a great deal of useful background information including the purpose of the book, the setting, the key verse and the key people.

c. In the **OVERVIEW** John found the description of the prophet's role most interesting, as well as the fact that the book of Isaiah is the first of the writings of the prophets in the Bible.

d. In the **BLUEPRINT** John noted the writings of Isaiah were divided into
   1. words of judgment chapters 1-39
   2. words of comfort chapters 40-66

e. In the **MEGATHEMES** John discovered the themes of holiness, punishment, salvation, Messiah and hope were contained within.

John read all the material in each of the above features and decided he would construct an outline presenting the book of Isaiah as

1. a book that is both a warning and a source of consolation to us, because it contains words of judgment (chapters 1-39) and words of comfort (chapters 40-66). It's key purpose being to call the nation of Judah back to God for God's salvation was coming through the Messiah.
2. a testament that reveals God's plan of redemption, announced and described 600 years before the coming of the Messiah. The key chapter is Isaiah 53.

3. a letter of invitation that calls us to return, repent, be renewed, trust God's redemption through the Messiah and rejoice because your Savior has come and is coming again.

HOME STUDY CHALLENGE

Using the example outline on the previous page as a pattern:

1. Start by selecting a book of the Bible
2. Turn to the pages preceding the first chapter
3. Read all the information given
   a. the **Timeline** across the top of the page
   b. the **Vital Statistics** found in the right or left hand margin of the first page
   c. the **Overview or general introduction** which begins on the first page next to the vital statistics
   d. the **Blueprint** follows the overview and precedes megathemes
   e. the **Megathemes** listed before the beginning of the first chapter
4. From the book you selected list 3 or 4 features you would choose to prepare a teaching outline.
5. Write down what you believe to be the most important information from those features, along with your reflections and comments.

I selected the Book of

____

I plan to use the following features to prepare my teaching outline:

____

____

The following is the information I feel is important to share:

____

____

____

____

____

____

CHAPTER 5 EXPLORING FEATURES OF SPECIAL INTEREST

The focus of this chapter entitled **Features of Special Interest** is to provide you with knowledge of and a reference to some of the extremely rich and important charts, outlines footnotes and other features contained in the Life Application Bible. Finding these features on your own would ordinarily take months or years of casual reading and study to discover. You are encouraged to take extensive notes as these features are presented so you will have a personal list to refer to and share with your church community.

SECTION 1 THE TEMPTATIONS

A combination chart and footnote study
The chart and footnotes provide a wealth of information regarding the temptations of Jesus as well as many insights for personal application.

1. Locate the chart entitled The Temptations found in Matthew 4
2. Read through the chart and the footnote on Matthew 4:1-10
3. Consider and answer the following questions:
   a. Why is it important to study the temptations of Jesus?

      ____

      ____

      ____

   b. Write down what point or points would you consider most important to share with others?

      ____

      ____

      ____

   c. How can understanding these points help them?

      ____

      ____

      ____

      ____

POSSIBLE ANSWERS TO THE QUESTIONS

(a) It is important because we experience the same temptations today and we need to know how to recognize them and overcome them.

(b) Answers may vary but one of the most important points is recognizing that the great weapon used to repel temptation is the Word of God.

(c) We can come to a realization that knowing and studying the Word of God personally is indispensable in overcoming the temptations of Satan. We can study and be prepared to resist when tempted by our own desires or the influence of the world.

ADDITIONAL INSIGHTS

The information puts into perspective the areas in which Satan tempted Jesus and how He responded to each temptation by using the Word of God. **Everyone is subject to temptation**, but we have hope of overcoming temptation because of Jesus, who has been tempted in all things yet did not sin, and because He promises to never leave us or forsake us. The chart lays out for us:

1. The form the temptation takes
2. The basic human need it attempts to fill
3. The doubt and lack of trust it reveals
4. The area of weakness Satan seeks to attack
5. The great weapon used to repel the attack

IMPORTANT FOOTNOTES

There are 14 footnotes in **Mt. 4:1 through Mt. 4:11** which provide extensive information about the temptations of Jesus as well as personal life application insights that will enhance any teaching or Bible study. The footnote on **Matthew 4:1-10** is especially helpful as it describes the temptations we face every day. A related footnote is found in **1 John 2:15-16**. This chart and the footnotes help us to understand not only the ways that Satan will try to tempt us, but more importantly the way to overcome the temptation by knowing and applying the Word of God.

GOD IS FAITHFUL EVEN WHEN WE DON'T UNDERSTAND THE TRIALS WE ARE GOING THROUGH.

During World War II a young flyer was shot down in the Pacific Ocean. He was able to make his way to a small deserted island. Being a Christian he thanked God for his deliverance and began to pray to be rescued. A few days passed and there was no rescue. With fervent prayers he cried out to God and at the same time built a small hut to live in. The following day a storm blew over the island and destroyed the hut. Discouraged he continued to pray, not understanding why God allowed the storm. Later that week he rebuilt the hut and made a small fire to cook with. While he was away gathering food a spark from the campfire ignited the hut. He saw smoke but by the time he got back the shelter had burned to the ground. On the brink of despair he wept and cried out to God for help. The next morning when he woke up he looked on the horizon and saw a ship. It drew closer; a lifeboat was lowered down and approached the beach. The captain greeted him. He said, "Son, you are a fortunate man. No ship ever goes by this island. But a few days ago a strong storm came up and blew us off course and just yesterday we saw your signal fire. You are fortunate indeed to be rescued."

***Are you going through a storm or through trials by fire?** God has not forsaken you. He is faithful to His Word, Romans 8:28, God is shaping all things to work together for the good of those who love Him and are called according to His purpose. Look up and trust God. Your deliverance is at hand. Stand firm on His Word, He will not fail you.*

STUDY GUIDE #8 WHEN TRIALS COME

Wherever we travel around the world brothers and sisters in the Lord are experiencing trials of many kinds. God stands ready with help from His Spirit and the counsel of His Word. Whatever the storm you are experiencing, God has a place in His Word for you to stand firm, a scripture passage or several passages, that you can rely on as the trial or storm rages. In a storm, when the floodwaters are rising, the people who survive are those who found a solid place to stand. His word is your place to stand, it's His promise to you, His counsel, and His comfort in your situation.

The following study guide will help you locate and receive some of the promises and counsel of God's word. Found in the Life Application Bible. <u>Take time to read the related footnotes for more wisdom and insights.</u>

	When trials come don't yield to despair or depression, don't wallow in self-pity, turn your face to the Lord for He has a plan.
Heb 13:5	Recall to mind His promises to you, you are His beloved child.
Isaiah 49:15-16	He said, I will never leave you or forsake you. Even if a mother could forget her infant, be without tenderness for the child of her womb, still I will not forget you. See upon the palms of my hands I have written your name.
Romans 8:28	Remember that in His plan God is shaping all things to work together for the good of those who love Him. We don't always see the wisdom of why things happen the way they do.
1 Cor 13:9	Our knowledge is yet imperfect and we yet see as through
1 Cor 13:12	a glass dimly. We still walk by faith and not by sight. We are
2 Cor 5:7	called to trust in the Lord with all our hearts and not rely on our

Prov 3:5-6 understanding. As we are mindful of Him
in all things He makes straight our path.
As we pray to the Lord for spiritual
growth, we can expect trials to come, for
endurance and maturity come through
trials. We realize
James 1:2-4 that when our faith is tested this makes for
endurance and
1 Cor 10:13 endurance comes to its perfection so that
we may be fully mature
and lacking in nothing. We know our God
will not let us be tested beyond our
2 Cor 12:9-10 strength and we know for us, as for the
apostle Paul, His grace will be sufficient
for every need. At the times we feel the
weakest, in Him we are made strong.
If the adversary tries to turn trial into
temptation we instinctively
Ephesians 6:10-17 put on the whole armor of our God. We
stand fast with the truth as the belt around
our waist, justice as our breastplate and
zeal to propagate the gospel as our
footgear. In all circumstances we hold up
faith before us as our shield that helps us to
extinguish the fiery darts of the evil one.
We put on the helmet of salvation and we
take up the sword of the Spirit, which is
the Word of God, against him.
James 4:7 We know if we resist the enemy he will
flee from us and
Romans 5:20 we are ever confident that as sin abounds
God's grace will abound more.
In times of trial or temptation we don't
dwell on the situation but
Col 3:1-4 on the victory. We set our minds and
hearts on what pertains to higher realms
where Christ is seated at God's right hand

and we become intent on things above rather than on things of earth.

We know that trials will come and go and the Lord will see us through them all,

Phil 3:13-16 — so we give no thought to what lies behind but push on to what is ahead. Our entire attention is on the finish line as we run toward the prize to which God calls, life on high in Christ Jesus. All of us who are spiritually mature must have this attitude. If you see it another way God will clarify it for you. It is important that we continue on our course no matter what stage we have reached. And our hearts cry AMEN!

The following charts provide additional resources and wisdom in times of trial. Be sure to read all related footnotes for more information

- **WHY WE DON'T GIVE UP** (1 Corinthians 10)
  Provides suggestions and direction when you are going through trials.
- **7 REASONS NOT TO WORRY** (Matthew 6)
- **WHERE TO GET HELP IN THE PSALMS**
  (after Psalm 150)
- **JESUS' MIRACLES** (located between the book of John and the book of Acts)
  Whatever you are going through, Jesus is still a miracle worker.
- **TROUBLES AND COMPLAINTS IN PSALMS**
  A source of inspiration and help when praying through trials.

THE FOLLOWING CHARTS LIST SOME OF THE NAMES OF THE LORD AND THE NAMES OF GOD

In times of trial the Names of the Lord express His unfailing commitment to save, rescue, protect, provide for and deliver His people. (The Name of the Lord is a strong tower. The righteousness run to it and they are saved Proverbs 18:10)

- **NAMES OF GOD** (Joshua 24...or Ruth 4 or 1 Kings 22)
- **NAMES OF THE MESSIAH** (Isaiah 9)
- **NAMES OF JESUS** (John 10)
- **NAMES OF JESUS** (Revelation 3)
- **REVIEW HEBREWS 11** (THE HALL OF FAITH)
  In times of adversity and trial the people of God stand strong in faith.
  Take time to read Hebrews 11 along with the related footnotes and be encouraged by the faith of those who have gone before us, men and women of God who persevered in trial and won the victory (Additional inspiration can be found in the Personality Profiles of these and other Bible characters. These profiles are listed in the Index to Personality Profiles, the very last of the four major indexes found after the book of Revelation).
- **RESORT TO THE POWER OF PRAYER**
  In adversity the following charts will inspire you.
  1. **HOW NEHEMIAH USED PRAYER** (Nehemiah 2)
  2. **PRAYER IN THE PSALMS** (Psalm 80)
- **IN TRIALS, TROUBLES AND PROBLEMS USE FOOTNOTES RESOURCES**
  Many of the footnotes contain wisdom that can be helpful in times of trial.
  Note the following example:
  Hannah's discouragement 1 Samuel chapters 1& 2
  Read these chapters along with the accompanying footnotes. Take special notice of 1 Samuel 1:8 and the footnote that describes how Hannah overcame discouragement.
  In the Index to Notes more wisdom like this can be found by researching the eight scripture listings and footnotes found under the topic "**TROUBLES**" and the seventy-nine listings found under the topic "**PROBLEMS**". Record and mark your favorites for future reference and use.

As you study the Life Application Bible add to this list the scripture passages, charts and footnotes you discover that will help you and others stand strong when trials come.

WHEN TRIALS COME…THE CRASH IN CURACAO
On the way to conduct a Life Application Bible Seminar on the island of Curacao, Netherlands Antilles, a drunk driver drove into the Ford pick-up truck we were riding in. The crash sent us into a high voltage electric pole that was sheared off and came down on the top of our truck. After we hit the electric pole the truck careened down a bank and came to a halt when it struck a concrete wall. The electric flashed all around us. The pick-up truck was a crew cab with fours doors. The wires were covering every door but one. God will make a way where there seems to be no way. He made a way for us to get out safely. We were shaken up a bit, but by the grace of God were unhurt. We continued on to the seminar. When we arrived we were cheered on by the three hundred and fifty students who had already heard about the accident and were interceding for us in prayer. Tremendous joy filled the meeting that night as we shared the riches of the Life Application Bible and thanked the Lord for His protection and deliverance. Ps 121:8 says I will protect your going out and coming in now and forever more.

Hosanna Christian Fellowship
Salina, Curacao
March 25, 2006 thru April 1, 2006

CHAPTER 5

SECTION 2 OUR TRUE IDENTITY IN CHRIST

The focus of this study is to explore a rich special feature chart entitled Our True Identity in Christ. Through this study you will discover some insights from God's Word about who we are in Christ. *We are justified, declared not guilty of sin; sanctified, made holy in Jesus Christ; new creations; blessed with every spiritual blessing in Christ; adopted as God's children; marked as belonging to God by the Holy Spirit; members of Christ's body, the Church and more.*

For now we will look at one key aspect of our true identity. We are forgiven of our sins and declared not guilty. Unless each of us understands and accepts the fullness of forgiveness through the sacrifice of Jesus, we cannot truly know who we are in Him or experience His new life. We run the risk of being confused, believing Satan's lies and being ineffective in God's work. These passages are not only informational but transformational.

Consider being in this situation: you realize that although the people in your congregation have accepted Jesus as their personal Lord and Savior, some of them still labor under the guilt and condemnation of their past sins. You may use this chart to help them come to understand their true identity in Christ and the freedom this brings.

a. Note the chart on the next page is also found between Ephesians 2 and Ephesians 3 in your Life Application Bible.

b. Take time to review the 24 choices listed.

c. Write down 1 or 2 passages to include in your presentation or sharing.

____

____

____

____

d. Research the ones you have chosen by reading the passages. Also read the related footnotes and use those footnotes that support your theme.

e. Write down what references you selected and why.

Our True Identity in Christ

Romans 3:24	We are justified (declared "not guilty of sin").
Romans 8:1	No condemnation awaits us.
Romans 8:2	We are set free from the law of sin and death.
1 Corinthians 1:2	We are sanctified (made holy) in Jesus Christ.
1 Corinthians 1:30	We are pure and holy in Christ.
1 Corinthians 15:22	We will be made alive at the resurrection.
2 Corinthians 5:17	We are new persons.
2 Corinthians 5:21	We are made right with God.
Galatians 3:28	We are one in Christ with all other believers.
Ephesians 1:3	We are blessed with every spiritual blessing.

Ephesians 1:4	We are holy and without fault.
Ephesians 1:5,6	We are adopted as God's children.
Ephesians 1:7	Our sins are taken away, and we are forgiven.
Ephesians 1:10,11	We will be brought under Christ's authority.
Ephesians 1:13	We are marked as belonging to God by the Holy Spirit.
Ephesians 2:6	We have been raised up to sit with Christ in the heavenly realms.
Ephesians 2:10	We are God's masterpieces.
Ephesians 2:13	We have been brought near to God.
Ephesians 3:6	We share in the promise through Christ.
Ephesians 3:12	We can come with freedom and confidence into God's presence.
Ephesians 5:29,30	We are members of Christ's body, the church.
Colossians 2:10	We have been given fullness in Christ.
Colossians 2:11	We are set free from our sinful nature.
2 Timothy 2:10	We will have eternal glory.

COMPLETED EXAMPLE: Patti selected the following points for her presentation:

1. Our sins are taken away and we are forgiven (by the power of the blood)
   Ephesians 1:7 In Him we have redemption through His blood, the forgiveness of (all our) sins...
2. We are declared "not guilty".
   Romans 3:24 Just as all have sinned and fall short of the glory of God, all are justified freely by His grace through the redemption that came by Christ Jesus.
3. No condemnation awaits us and we are set free from the law of sin and death.
   Romans 8:1-2 Therefore, there is now no condemnation for those who are in Christ Jesus, because through Jesus Christ the law of the Spirit of life set me free from the law of sin and death.
4. We are sanctified (set apart) and made (holy and) acceptable in Jesus Christ
   1 Corinthians 1:2...to those sanctified in Christ Jesus and called to be holy....

Take note: the above-completed example can be used as a pattern for you to present other themes from this chart. It is a type of teaching outline you could use in a Bible study or Sunday school lesson. After each point you could add your own comments and reflections or discussion questions.

STUDY GUIDE # 9
GOD TAKES THE INITIATIVE IN THE LIVES OF HIS PEOPLE
SHATTERING THE WEDGE OF DISCOURAGEMENT
WITH THE HAMMER OF HIS WORD

Remember, God is the initiator of whole plan of salvation in all its aspects.
The following information will help you discover how God will carry on the good work He has started in you right up to the day of His return. When you are down, depressed and discouraged you must realize the wedge of discouragement is one of the enemy's greatest tools, like a heavy rock weighing upon you. You may feel like giving up or loosing hope. It is then that you call upon the Lord and turn to His Word.
Although the wedge of discouragement is like a heavy rock, God says in Jeremiah 23:29 'is not My Word like a hammer that shatters rock'. **You must grasp this great truth, the hammer of God's word can shatter rocks of discouragement in your life.** For each rock He has a Word hammer to shatter it. The following is a list of some of them. They will lift you up and encourage you. God will speak to you in the Scripture and in the footnotes. You will come to **realize when you feel helpless God will take the initiative.** He will help you, deliver you, reach your heart with His powerful Word, break the discouragement and give you a new, positive perspective on life. The insights below can help you walk in victory.

*****Be sure to read the complete scripture passage and footnote for each reference given.

Psalm 4:3 You have been set apart for God, He will hear when you call

- Footnote: *if you have trusted Christ for salvation God has forgiven you and He will listen when you call. Look at your problems in the light of God's power instead of looking at God in the shadow of your problems.*

Philippians 1:6 You are Christians under construction

- 1st Footnote: *God will take the initiative.*

The God who began a good work within you continues it throughout your life.

- 2nd Footnote: *When God starts a project He completes it when you are discouraged, remember, God won't give up on you.*

2 Corinthians 12:7-9 Your weakness plus God's grace can release God's power in you

- Footnote: (2 Corinthians 12:9) *Take courage, God can demonstrate and display His power in weak people. We can rely on Him for our strength and effectiveness*

2 Corinthians. 3:18 The Holy Spirit is at work within you

- Footnote:
  - *a. The truth about Christ in the Good News transforms you over time*
  - *b. As you grow in this knowledge the Holy Spirit helps you change*
  - *c. Becoming Christ-like is a progressive experience*

Romans 8:28 God is working behind the scenes for your good

- Footnote: *God is able to turn every circumstance around for your long-range good. Therefore, you need to receive this new perspective and new mindset.*

1 John 1:9 God is a forgiver and a cleanser of all sin

- Footnote:

  You must rely on His power to forgive and overcome all your sins

  You must open your hearts to grasp what He has already done

Psalm 51:10 God is able to cleanse and renew, you cannot do it on your own

- Footnote: *Grasp what God can do in you*

Ezekiel 36:25-27 Get ready to receive. God desires to cleanse and give a new heart and a new spirit

- Footnote: *God's plan a fresh start, physical and spiritual restoration, transformation and empowerment*

Psalm 37:23-24 You can count on God to personally direct your life

- Footnote: *Receive this in your heart and mind. God is actively guiding, watching over and making your steps firm.*

Jeremiah 29:11-14 God has a great plan for your future, a future full of hope and prosperity

- Footnote: Jeremiah 29:11 *God knows your future, provides what you need and goes with you.*
- Footnote: Jeremiah 29:12-14 *Through new beginnings and a new purpose God can bring about a new person.*

Ephesians 1:18-20 Trust that the tremendous power of the Holy Spirit is at work in you

- Footnote: Ephesians 1:19-20 *God's incomparable power is available now.*

1 John 2:26-27 Be encouraged God will take the initiative to teach you through the Holy Spirit

- Footnote: *With the God-inspired Scriptures and the Holy Spirit anointing we will be able to discern truth from error.*
- Footnote: *Jesus lives in us through the Holy Spirit. He, working in you, will give you guidance and strength. You can count on it.*

Galatians 5:22-23 The fruit of the Holy Spirit will spring up in you

- Footnote: (22-23) *The Holy Spirit's spontaneous work will produce fruit in you, the same fruit found in the nature of Christ.*

Philippians 4:13 Impossible things are made possible through Christ's strength in you

- Footnote: *There is power to face all types of challenges when you are in union with Christ.*

Philippians 4:19 You can trust God to meet your needs

- Footnote: *He will meet all types of needs, especially provision and power to live for Him.*

Chart research
Take time to read through each of these charts, the Scripture passages given and the accompanying footnotes.

1. **God Uses Ordinary People (located Judges 6)**
   God will work within you and use you just as you are, with all your faults, shortcomings and flaws. Note the people listed and how they were used by God in the past. Now step out and trust Him with your life.
2. **Our True Identity in Christ (located between Ephesians 1 & 3)**
   As a believer, *what God has accomplished through Jesus has changed your identity*. You are no longer under the curse, dead in your sins, lost and without hope. No you are…(read the chart)

***Using the pattern of these encouraging passages, charts and footnotes we urge you to add to this list as you read and discover more great truths in the Life Application Bible.

CHAPTER 5

SECTION 3 THE SECTION OF GREAT RICHES

In this study we will take time to become familiar with **seven unbelievably rich and useful charts** relating to the life and ministry of Jesus.

Located between the gospel of John and the book of Acts, this section contains several charts of special interest. Many of the charts are preceded by a helpful and informative introduction. Looking at the first three charts, notice that there are 250 events in the life of Christ. These events are listed in a harmony of the gospels. The titles of these charts are:

1. Birth and Preparation of Jesus Christ
2. Message and Ministry of Jesus Christ
3. Death and Resurrection of Jesus Christ

The additional charts that provide supplementary information are:

4. The Parables of Jesus
5. Jesus' Miracles
6. Comparison of the Four Gospels
7. Messianic Prophecies and Fulfillments

To grow in understanding and experience in using these charts we suggest the following:

a. Turn to the above charts found between John and Acts in your Life Application Bible.
b. Take a few minutes to review the seven charts and mark this section with a Post-It-Note
c. Select your favorite chart.
d. Write down what chart you selected and why you selected it.

____

____

____

e. In what ways could you use this chart or these charts to spread the Gospel or teach others about Christ?

f. What other ways could these charts be used to enrich those in your church?

CHAPTER 5

SECTION 3 THE SECTION OF GREAT RICHES

SUGGESTIONS:

- One person suggested making copies of the chart entitled Messianic Prophecies and Their Fulfillment to present in a weekly Bible study that would allow plenty of time for questions and discussion.
- A pastor, using the chart entitled The Birth and Preparation of Jesus Christ, selected and preached on a different event each week leading up to the celebration of Christmas. He also used the chart entitled Death and Resurrection of Jesus Christ in the same step-by-step manner leading up to the celebration of Easter.
- A church member, who is part of a hospital visitation team, suggested that the chart on the Miracles of Jesus could be shared with sick or suffering members of the church as a way of encouraging them and strengthening their faith.

It is important to spend time exploring ways of presenting and using these charts that go beyond personal study so that others would receive the benefit of these great riches.
Write your thoughts here.

____

____

____

____

____

____

____

____

____

____

____

____

CHAPTER 5

SECTION 4 NAMES OF THE LORD CHARTS

The focus of this study is to become aware of and familiar with the four rich charts that contain lists of the names of the Lord and insights into each name. These are excellent charts for improving and enhancing our personal relationship with Jesus through a study of the Names of God.

Here are the names of the four charts and their location in the Life Application Bible.

NOTE: Each chart gives chapter and verse reference:

(1) located in Joshua 24, (or Ruth 4 or 1 Kings 22) consists of 16 of the Hebrew Names of God, their meaning and their significance (if you cannot find this chart in Joshua 24 check the Index to Charts in your Life Application Bible).

(2) located in Isaiah 9, contains four of the Names of the Messiah which have special meaning and a description of each.

(3) located in John 10, reveals 8 of the Names of Jesus and their significance.

(4) located in Revelations 3, is comprised of 19 Names of Jesus, each one tells something of His character and highlights a particular aspect of His role within God's plan of redemption.

Consider being in this situation: You are speaking to a class of new believers. You realize that their perception of God is incomplete. Your desire is to help them learn about the Names of God, and the significance and importance of His Names, so that their trust in Him and their relationship with Him will grow. Review the four charts

a. Select 2 or 3 names that you feel would be important for them to understand and appropriate.

b. Read the Scripture reference and, if there is one, the related footnote.

c. Write down the names you selected, the Scripture reference, along with the meaning and/or the significance of each.

d. Explain why you selected these names.

e. If one of these names has had an impact on your life and personal relationship with the Lord write a short summary.

CHAPTER 5

SECTION 4 NAMES OF THE LORD CHARTS

COMPLETED EXAMPLE: Realizing the great need of many new believers to know and experience the Lord's peace, presence and power, Jim chose four names of God from the list in Joshua 24. (or Ruth 4 or 1 Kings 22)

1. Yahweh Shalom--The Lord is Peace--Judges 6:24
   God gives us peace, so we need not fear.
2. Yahweh Shammah--The Lord is There--Ezekiel 48:35
   God is always present with us.
3. Yahweh Sabaoth--Lord of Hosts--1 Samuel 1:3--God is our Savior and
   Isaiah 6:1-3 God is our protector.
4. El Shaddai--God Almighty--Genesis 17:1 and Psalm 91:1
   God is all-powerful

Jim wrote how Yahweh Shalom had a special meaning to him since it was God who brought a great peace into his life, a peace he had not experienced before, a peace that passes understanding.

APPLICATION

A. One pastor suggested a study or exposition of only one or two names per week, so that church members have time to fully reflect and receive the most out of each name, applying it personally.
For instance: Jesus is not just the ***Good Shepherd,*** but He is my personal Shepherd, leading and guiding me everyday. Jesus is not just the ***Prince of Peace,*** He is my personal source of peace, the peace that passes understanding, the peace that the world cannot give nor take away.

B. A Bible study leader suggested it is important to study, know and use the wonderful Names of the Lord as we proclaim and minister the Gospel because the Names of the Lord reveal:

1. **The Person of God** (revealing who God is)
2. **The Power of God** (revealing what He is able to do)
3. **The Plan of God** (revealing what He desires to do)
4. **The Promise of God** (revealing what we can trust Him to bring about)

What other applications can you think of? Write your reflections here.

____

____

____

____

For further understanding of the various facets of God's character we recommend the chart "HOW GOD IS DESCRIBED IN THE PSALMS" located in Psalm 104.

At a Bible study where the Names of the Lord were being studied and appreciated a sense of joy and praise started to develop and grow. As an expression of the joy all at the Bible study sang with great enthusiasm the song
The Name of the Lord is a strong tower.
The righteous run into it and they are saved.
Oh, the Name of the Lord is a strong tower.
The righteous run into it and they are saved.
Blessed be the Name of the Lord.
Blessed be the Name of the Lord.
Blessed be the Name of the Lord Most High.
The Name of the Lord is a strong tower.
The righteous run into it and they are saved.
Oh, the Name of the Lord is a strong tower.
The righteous run into it and they are saved.
Blessed be the Name of the Lord.
Blessed be the Name of the Lord.
Blessed be the Name of the Lord Most High.

CHAPTER 5

SECTION 5 APPLYING WHAT HAS BEEN LEARNED HOME STUDY CHALLENGE

PREPARING A TEACHING OUTLINE ON THE SUBJECT OF *FAITH*

The focus of this study is to help you apply the lessons you have learned.

Suppose you have been asked to present a teaching on the subject of faith. Start by constructing an outline. You may choose any feature or combination of features in the Life Application Bible.

a. List the feature or features you chose for your outline

____

____

____

____

b. Record the main theme of your outline.

____

____

____

____

c. Write down the points you would use to develop your theme.

____

____

*****Take note of the completed example below.**

a. A Bible study leader chose the feature Charts.
He turned to the Index to Charts and located the chart entitled
Faith That Works in James 5.

b. He recorded the main theme of his outline from this chart
Your Faith Must Express Itself in Actions James 2:14-16

c. He used the following points from the chart to develop his theme.

- Be merciful to others, as God is merciful to you. James 2:13
- Blessed are the peacemakers; they plan in peace and reap a harvest of goodness James 3:17-18
- Don't speak evil against each other. If you do, you are criticizing God's law. James 4:11
- Be patient in suffering, as God's prophets were patient. James 5:10
- Be honest in your speech; just say a simple yes or no so that you will not sin. James 5:12

*****Another Completed Example.**

a. A Bible college student's research led him to the Index to Notes.

b. Under the heading of faith, he chose the theme Why Does God Save By Faith Alone? Romans 3:28 (Justification By Faith)

c. He read the passage and felt that the four points he found in the footnote were ideal for his teaching outline.
   - Faith eliminates the pride of human effort, because faith is not a deed that we do.
   - Faith exalts what God has done, not what we do.
   - Faith admits that we can't keep the law or measure up to God's standards-
     we need help.
   - Faith is based on our relationship with God, not our performance for God.

The completed examples above can be used as patterns for creating your own teaching outline on any subject. To enhance and develop your outline, add your own reflections, illustrations and personal experience.

STUDY GUIDE #10 CHARTS THAT ENCOURAGE SPIRITUAL GROWTH

Wherever we travel teaching brothers and sisters in Christ how to use this wonderful tool we are always asked what we can suggest for further study using the Life Application Bible. Following is a list of a few of the best and most interesting charts we have found. It is a list that will whet your appetite for more. These charts would ordinarily take months of casual reading to discover. Our hope is that upon reading them you will be encouraged to create your own list of favorites. Charts that have key importance to you will be the ones you will find easy to share and communicate with others.

These charts can also be located by using the Index to Charts that is found in the back of the Life Application Bible after the book of Revelations. IT IS MOST IMPORTANT TO REMEMBER to read all the footnotes related to the chart you are studying. If a scripture reference is given in the chart, read the footnote for that scripture as well.

PRAYER CHARTS

There are three key charts that provide help in deepening our prayer lives.

1. **HOW NEHEMIAH USED PRAYER**
   Located in Nehemiah 2. This chart lists (a)seven occasions in which Nehemiah used prayer, (b)the summary of his prayer, (c)what it accomplished, (d)reflections for life application and (e)Scripture references. This chart would be a great addition for any study on prayer.
2. **PRAYER IN THE PSALMS**
   Located in Psalm 80. This chart contains some excellent insights about the book of Psalms and explains how honesty, openness and sincerity are valuable to God. A study of this chart can enrich our personal experience of prayer. Scripture references are included.
3. **HOW TO PRAY FOR OTHER CHRISTIANS**
   Located in Colossians 1. This chart is based on the apostle Paul's prayer. It contains seven insights that will help us pray for other believers, along with the Scripture reference for each. It relates (a) the perspective of his prayer—thankfulness; (b) the priority of his prayer—spiritual needs; and (c) the power source of his prayer—God.

REFERENCE CHARTS

The following is a list of some of the most useful and important Old Testament reference charts found in the Life Application Bible.

1. **THE OFFERINGS**
   Located in Leviticus 1. This chart lists the five key offerings the Israelites made to God: the Burnt Offering, the Grain Offering, the Peace Offering, the Sin Offering and the Guilt Offering. It also lists the purpose and significance of the offering compared to Christ the perfect offering. This chart along with the footnotes related to each scripture reference given is a great help in comparing the Old Testament offerings to Jesus, the perfect offering.
2. **THE FESTIVALS**
   Also called the Feasts. Located in Leviticus 23, this chart lists the nineteen days Israel celebrated as national holidays. Each feast is listed along with its scripture reference, what it celebrated and its importance. This chart and related footnotes gives us insights into the feasts Jesus lived and celebrated.
3. **GOD USES COMMON PEOPLE**
   Located in Judges 6. This chart contains a list of thirteen ordinary people who were used by God in extraordinary ways, the task they performed as well as the scripture reference. Reading the chart gives affirmation and encouragement to ordinary people who would dare to believe that God could use them to accomplish great things in His service.
4. **THE MIRACLES OF ELIJAH AND ELISHA**
   Located in 2 Kings 2. This chart lists seven miracles of Elijah and ten of Elisha, where they are found and the factors involved. The miracles show God's power is far greater than that of idols. This miracle power is available to us today through the Holy Spirit sent forth at Pentecost.
5. **WHO WERE THESE PROPHETS**
   Located in 2 Kings 17. This chart lists eighteen Old Testament prophets,when they ministered, during whose reign, their main message and thesignificance of the message. This chart is a great resource because each prophet's message has real meaning for us today. The words and the thoughts of the prophets still have the power to turn God's people back to Him.

6. **BIBLE PERSECUTIONS**
Located in 2 Chronicles 18. This chart lists twenty-five instances of persecution, the persecuted, the persecutors, why the persecution, and the result of the persecution along with scripture references. All who follow Jesus can expect persecution. Reading the stories and understanding the lessons learned through persecution can be a great preparation for our own walk of faith.

7. **GREAT REVIVALS IN THE BIBLE**
Located in 2 Chronicles 29. This chart lists eight revivals mentioned in the Old Testament. It names the leader of each revival, gives the scriptural references and relates how the people responded. These references provide great insights for those seeking personal revival or revival for their church.

8. **PSALMS IN DAVID'S LIFE**
Located in Psalm 5. This chart lists psalms connected with specific events in the life of David which show us an outline of his growing relationship with God. After studying the outline presented we can't help but contemplate the events of our own growing relationship with God and perhaps see some parallels.

9. **CHRIST IN THE PSALMS**
Located in Psalm 22. This chart can be a great faith builder. It lists eighteen references to Christ in the psalms as well as the passages in the New Testament where they are fulfilled. It can be an inspiring addition to a group Bible study.

10. **PSALMS TO LEARN AND LOVE**
Located in Psalm 23. This chart lists psalms worth learning and memorizing. As we memorize God's words we can be sure that the Holy Spirit (The Remembrancer) will bring them to mind at just the right time when we really need them.

11. **PSALMS THAT HAVE INSPIRED HYMNS**
The great words of God make great hymns.
Located in Psalm 47. This chart lists nine psalms and hymns they have inspired. A study of the psalm will give the related hymn a new depth of meaning.

12. WHERE TO GET HELP IN THE BOOK OF PSALMS

Located at the end of the book of Psalms, this chart contains an alphabetical list of important subjects followed by the psalm that relates to each.

For example: when you feel afraid turn to Psalm 3; 4; 27; 46; 49; 56; 91; 118.

This chart is a great help in locating and matching the counsel of God's Word with a particular life situation or need.

13. **A HARMONY OF THE GOSPELS**

Located after the Gospel of John, this chart contains two hundred and fifty events in the life of Christ found in the four gospels. This harmony combines the four gospels into a single, chronological account of Jesus' life on earth. This harmony will help you to better visualize the travels of Jesus, study the four gospels comparatively, and appreciate the unity of their message.

14. **THE MIRACLES OF JESUS**

Located between the Gospel of John and the Book of Acts, this chart list thirty five miracles of Jesus and where they are found in the gospels. The miracles reveal to us the power of God, the presence of God and the compassion of God. They provide excellent insight into God's care and love.

15. THE PARABLES OF JESUS

Located between the Gospel of John and the Book of Acts, this list is an excellent teaching tool that categorizes the parables into ten groupings in outline form.

CHAPTER 6 ADDITIONAL STUDY HELPS

ABBREVIATIONS OF THE BOOKS OF THE BIBLE OLD TESTAMENT

Genesis	Gen
Exodus	Exod
Leviticus	Lev
Numbers	Num
Deuteronomy	Deut
Joshua	Jos
Judges	Judg
Ruth	Ru
1 Samuel	1 Sm
2 Samuel	2 Sm
1 Kings	1 Kgs
2 Kings	2 Kgs
1 Chronicles	1 Chr
2 Chronicles	2 Chr
Ezra	Ezr
Nehemiah	Neh
Esther	Esth
Job	Job
Psalms	Ps
Proverbs	Prov
Ecclesiastes	Eccl
Song of Songs	Song
Isaiah	Isa
Jeremiah	Jer
Lamentations	Lam
Ezekiel	Ezek
Daniel	Dan
Hosea	Hos
Joel	Joel
Amos	Amos
Obadiah	Ob
Jonah	Jon
Micah	Mic
Nahum	Nah
Habakkuk	Hab
Zephaniah	Zeph
Haggai	Hag
Zechariah	Zech
Malachi	Mal

NEW TESTAMENT

Matthew	Matt
Mark	Mark
Luke	Luke
John	John
Acts	Acts
Romans	Rom
1 Corinthians	1 Cor
2 Corinthians	2 Cor
Galatians	Gal
Ephesians	Eph
Philippians	Phil
Colossians	Col
1 Thessalonians	1 Thes
2 Thessalonians	2 Thes
1 Timothy	1 Tim
2 Timothy	2 Tim
Titus	Titus
Philemon	Phlm
Hebrews	Heb
James	Jas
1 & 2 Peter	1 & 2 Pet
1 John	1 Jn
2 John	2 Jn
3 John	3 Jn
Jude	Jude
Revelation	Rev

GLOSSARY OF TERMS

Take time to review the list of terms in this book. It will help you to understand and grasp the definitions, concepts and words used within.

APPLICATION	Suggestions or insights on how to use or apply Scripture resources being studied.
BIBLE COLLEGE IN A BOOK	Name given to the Life Application Bible by pastors and teachers in developing countries.
COMPLETED EXAMPLE	The finished answer to a question, a proposed situation or study challenge in this book.
DEFINITION OF FEATURES	All definitions can be found in chapter four.
FAMILY OF BELIEVERS	Refers to other Christians around the world who love and study the Life Application Bible and are devoted to bringing it to the nations.
FEATURE	A feature is a study tool, a reference tool or teaching tool found in the Life Application Bible.
FN or NOTES	An abbreviation for footnotes.
THE FOUR PRINCIPLES	The four principles refer to the study method used to emphasize material in the Life Application Bible Seminar. Participants SEE the material on an overhead or in this book; they HEAR the information spoken by the teacher or leader; they WRITE the information in their notes to refer to later; and they SPEAK IT BACK by responding to the

	questions presented. All of these help participants remember the information given.
HOME STUDY CHALLENGE	An exercise or research project that can be completed as homework at another time.
LIFE APPLICATION BIBLE SEMINAR	Refers to the course we have used around the world to teach and instruct others how to use the Life Application Bible. This book is based on that course.
LARGE GROUP EXERCISE	Refers to using a study challenge in a large group situation where a number of people have gathered to study this course together.
PATTERN	Refers to a completed study outline or example given in this book that can be used as a guide or blueprint to assemble other outlines.
STUDY GUIDE	A Scripture resource tool, researched and developed through our own personal use and exploration of the Life Application Bible.
TESTIMONY	Telling the story of a personal experience or an encounter with the Lord. A witness of what God has done.

In this book there are ten key study guides to be used with the Life Application Bible.

They are categorized to provide immediate access to the riches found within. Following is:

A BRIEF SUMMARY OF THE LIFE APPLICATION BIBLE STUDY GUIDES

1. **USING THE LIFE APPLICATION BIBLE TO SHARE THE WONDERFUL MESSAGE OF SALVATION**
   Many have asked, "Can you tell us what are some Scripture passages, charts and footnotes from the Life Application Bible that we can use to understand God's gift of salvation and lead others to Christ?" In this study guide are some of the best from our research. Every Scripture passage has a key explanatory footnote. We encourage you to add to this list.

2. **ADDITIONAL FOOTNOTE RESEARCH**
   This study guide is a list of excellent Old Testament footnotes that contain numbered point-by-point teaching outlines. It can be helpful to pastors, teachers and anyone who prepares bible study lessons

3. **USING THE LIFE APPLICATION BIBLE AS A RESEARCH TOOL**
   The goal of this study guide is to give an example of how the Life Application Bible can be used as a research tool and to provide a sampling of some footnote information regarding the occult and occult practices. We created this study guide because we have continually encountered occult practices in our mission work around the world. We hope this study guide will be a catalyst for using the Life Application Bible to confront the deception and confusion found in these practices.

4. **THE JESUS STUDY GUIDE**
Pastors around the world have continually asked us for bible study material about Jesus. In response to this request we have compiled the following resources:

- Two hundred fifty-three Names of the Lord...those with supporting footnotes are designated FN
- The Prayers of Jesus with chapter and verse
- The Priesthood of Jesus with locations in Scripture
- Prophecies concerning the Messiah and their fulfillment with Old and New Testament locations
- Forty-five key charts about Jesus, His life and His ministry
This study guide can be of great value to you because it gives immediate access to information that could take months or years to find on your own.

5. **AN OVERVIEW OF THE FOUR MAJOR INDEXES AND DICTIONARY CONCORDANCE**
This study guide is a brief description of the key indexes in the Life Application Bible and where they are located. Using and understanding these indexes is a vital part of gathering material for teaching and personal study. There is also an explanation of the dictionary concordance.

6. **CHARTS ABOUT BIBLE PEOPLE**
This study guide contains seven rich charts about bible characters; where each chart is located and a brief description of its contents. These charts provide interesting and thought provoking information that can easily be adapted for use in sermons or bible study.

7. **DEFINITIONS OF FEATURES**
It has been our experience that many people have had difficulty understanding the features and terms found in the Life Application Bible. This study guide provides a simplified explanation of those features, defined and clarified. It also shows where the features are located in the Bible.

8. **WHEN TRIALS COME**
One of the greatest needs we see in the lives of people around the world is wisdom from God's Word to use when going through trials. Overcoming trials and difficulties in everyday life are a constant challenge. This study guide contains multiple pages of Scripture and wisdom from the Life Application Bible, including specific charts, topical headings, references to the names of God and more. This guide gives immediate access to resources like
   - 7 Reasons Not to Worry
   - Where to Get Help From the Psalms
   - How Nehemiah Used Prayer

9. **GOD TAKES THE INITIATIVE IN THE LIVES OF HIS PEOPLE**
The hammer of God's Word can shatter the rocks of discouragement (Jeremiah 23:29). This study guide contains a variety of Scripture, footnotes and charts that demonstrate how God takes the initiative in the lives of His people. When you feel like giving up or loosing hope it is then that you call upon the Lord and turn to His Word.

10. **CHARTS THAT ENCOURAGE SPIRITUAL GROWTH**
We are often asked if we can recommend anything for further study. This study guide is a list of some key charts on a variety of subjects. They are some of our favorites and most useful. We encourage you to create your own list of favorites.

IN DEPTH AND EXTENDED RESEARCH
GOING BEYOND THE BASICS

Many of our Christian friends around the world have a great hunger to probe the depths of God's Word for wisdom and understanding. They are not satisfied with knowing only a little about a subject or a topic in the Bible.

The following example is an attempt at doing a deeper study using the Life Application Bible alone. We realize many brothers and sisters have limited resources and access to Bible commentaries or other research materials, but they do have a Life Application Bible.

EXTENDED STUDY EXAMPLE ON THE SUBJECT OF SALVATION

The subject of salvation has already been touched on in Study Guide #1. We will now go beyond that resource.

- **Index to Notes**
  Looking at the listings in the Salvation Study Guide (Study Guide #1)
  Notice these listings are expanded upon in the Index to Notes (The Master Index). For example: in the Salvation Study Guide there are eight references on the subject of Repentance; in the Index to Notes there are twenty-nine. A deeper understanding of any subject can be found by researching all its listings in the Index to Notes.
- **Related Subjects**
  Studying Related Subjects can increase our knowledge and understanding of the main topic we have chosen. Related subjects provide an expanded view and another perspective of any given topic. For example…
  researching the words "grace" and "mercy" can help us to comprehend the depth of our salvation.
  Notice in the Index to Notes the related subject of
  ***Evangelism has thirteen references
  ***Good news/gospel has thirty-two references

***Witnessing has fifty-two references
***Spiritual rebirth has nine references
***Grace has seven references
***Mercy has seven references
Researching these related subjects adds to our knowledge of salvation

- **Charts and Personality Profiles**
  Take time to review any Charts or Personality Profiles that can give us new insights to our subject. Listed in the Index to Notes we find four charts under the subject of Salvation
  ***Salvation's Freeway
  ***What Has God Done About Sin?
  ***Salvation Through Faith
  ***From Death to Life
  There is also a Personality Profile...the profile of Nicodemus in the Gospel of John. A review of these charts and personality profiles will expand our grasp of salvation.
- **Cross References**
  Take time to research all Cross References. Found in the center margins, they give a related passage of Scripture located in another place in the Bible. Like stringing pearls, they connect great themes that extend throughout God's Word.
- **Dictionary Concordance**
  Finally, let us use the Dictionary Concordance, found in the back of the Life Application Bible, after the Index to Maps and Personality Profiles. This is not a complete concordance, but an abbreviated one. Some subjects are not covered, but it is still very useful. Remember, the concordance is set up like a dictionary. It lists subjects or topics in alphabetical order, gives a short definition of each topic and lists some of the chapter and verse references where the topic is used. The current Life Application Bible Concordance has thirty-three references that can help us learn more about the subject of salvation.

You can use this extended study example as a pattern to research any topic or subject in the Life Application Bible. The following is an outline of the study progression we used.

1. The Salvation Study Guide with limited references
2. The Index to Notes expanded resources
3. The Related Subjects List
4. Charts and Personality Profiles
5. Cross Reference information
6. The Dictionary Concordance

PRAY AND RELY ON GOD.
As you take out your Life Application Bible and all that you have learned from this book, remember to resort to the power of prayer when you face obstacles. You will never be overcome or defeated.

Watchman Nee, great Chinese evangelist and missionary, related this story:
During a preaching mission to an island off the South China coast preaching seemed quite fruitless. It was discovered that this it was because of the dedication of the people to an idol they called Ta-wang. They were convinced of his power because on the day of his festival and parade each year the weather was always perfect. Brother Wu, a new convert in the Lord, asked the people who were devoted to the idol, "When is the procession this year?" "It is fixed for January 11", was the reply. Then said Brother Wu, "I promise you that it will certainly rain on the 11th." There was an outburst from the crowd. "That's enough, we don't want to hear anymore preaching. If there is rain on the 11th then your God is God!"

Watchman Nee had been elsewhere in the village when this confrontation had taken place. Realizing the situation was serious he called his missionaries to prayer. On the morning of the 11th there was not a cloud in the sky. As they prayed over their breakfast sprinkles of rain began to fall followed by heavy rain.

The worshippers of the idol Ta-wang were so upset they placed it in a chair and carried it outdoors, hoping this would stop the rain. But the rain increased. After carrying the idol a short distance the carriers stumbled and fell, dropping the idol and fracturing its jaw and left arm. A number of young people turned to Christ as a result of the rain coming in answer to prayer. But the elders of the village made divination and said the wrong day had been chosen. The proper day of the day of the procession should have been the 14th. When Nee and his friends heard this, they again went to prayer asking for rain on the 14th and for clear days for preaching until then. That afternoon the skies cleared and on the good days that followed there were thirty converts. On the crucial day of the test, the 14th started as another perfect day. As the evening approached and the appointed hour for the idol to be acknowledged, the missionaries quietly prayed and brought the matter to the Lord's remembrance. Not a minute late, His answer came with torrential rains and floods. The power of the idol over the islanders was broken. The enemy defeated. Believing prayer had brought the victory. Conversions followed and the Christian workers who had witnessed His power continued their work with confidence.

Victory Verses From the Psalms

Psalm 1:1-3

Oh, the joys of those who do not follow the advice of the wicked, or stand around with sinners, or join in with scoffers. But they delight in the law of the Lord; and meditate on his law day and night. They are like trees planted by the water bearing fruit each season without fail. Their leaves never wither, and whatever they do prospers.

Psalm 18:2

The LORD is my rock, my fortress, and my savior; my God is my rock, in whom I find protection. He is my shield, the strength of my salvation, and my stronghold.

Psalm 18:30

As for God, his way is perfect. All the LORD's promises prove true. He is a shield for all who look to him for protection.

Psalm 23:3-4

He renews my strength. He guides me along right paths, bringing honor to his name.
Even when I walk through the dark valley of death,
I will not be afraid, for you are close beside me.
Your rod and your staff protect and comfort me.

Psalm 27:14
Wait patiently for the LORD. Be brave and courageous. Yes, wait patiently for the LORD.

PSALM 31:3
You are my rock and my fortress. For the honor of your name, lead me out of this peril.

Psalm 31:24
So be strong and take courage, all you who put your hope in the LORD!

Psalm 32:1-2
Oh, what joy for those whose disobedience is forgiven, whose sin is put out of sight! Yes, what joy for those whose sin is no longer counted against them by the Lord.

Psalm 32:8
The LORD says, "I will guide you along the best pathway for your life. I will advise you and watch over you."

Psalm 34:19
Many are the afflictions of the righteous, but the Lord delivers him out of them all.

Psalm 37:23
The steps of the godly are directed by the LORD. He delights in every detail of their lives.

Psalm 40:2
He lifted me out of the pit of despair, out of the mud and the mire. He set my feet on solid ground and steadied me as I walked along.

Psalm 42:8
Through each day the LORD pours his unfailing love upon me, and through each night I sing his songs, praying to God who gives me life.

Psalm 46:1
God is our refuge and strength, an ever-present help in time of trouble.

Psalm 55:22
Give your burdens to the LORD, and he will take care of you.
He will not permit the godly to slip and fall.

Psalm 56:3-4
But when I am afraid, I put my trust in you.
O God, I praise your word. I trust in God, so why should I be afraid?

Psalm 68:19
Praise the Lord; praise God our savior! For each day he carries us in his arms.

Psalm 73:28
But as for me, how good it is to be near God! I have made the Sovereign LORD my shelter, and I will tell everyone about the wonderful things you did.

Psalm 86:5
O Lord, you are so good, so ready to forgive, so full of unfailing love for all who ask your aid.

Psalm 103:12
As far as the east is from the west has he put our transgressions from us.

Psalm 107:20
He sent forth His Word and he healed them. He delivered them from destruction.

Psalm 119:11
I have hidden your word in my heart, so that I might not sin against you.

Psalm 119:25
I lie prostrate in the dust. Revive me by your word.

Psalm 119:28
I am sad and tired; make me strong again by your word like you have promised.

Psalm 119:50
Remember what you told me, your servant. I hang on to these words for dear life. These words hold me up in bad times. Your word gives me life.

Psalm 119:89
Forever, O LORD, your word is established in heaven.

Psalm 119:105
Your word is a lamp for my feet and a light for my path.

Psalm 121:1-2
I look up to the mountains—Does my help come from the mountains? No, my strength comes from God Who made heaven and earth and the mountains.

Psalm 138:7
Though I am surrounded by troubles, you will preserve me against the anger of my enemies. You will clench your fist against my angry enemies! Your power will save me.

We pray that the information you have studied in this book and the Life Application Bible will continue to be a blessing in your life and the lives of those you touch.

For more copies of this book please contact us at our website www.lifeapplicationbibleseminar.com

Serving an Awesome God
Jim and Patti Moffett